# The LETSaholic Twist

Everything you always wanted to know about LETS

but did not know who to ask

**James Taris**

First published in China in 2005 by James Taris.
Reprinted 2020

Cover and book layout designs by James Taris.

For permission to publish any part of this book please send your request to:
JamesTaris@gmail.com

# CONTENTS

## Chapter 4 – Wants

## Chapter 5 – Trading

## Chapter 6 – Administration Help

## Chapter 9 – Image

## Chapter 10 – Committee Roles

# CHAPTER 1

## Birth of a LETSaholic

*"Every generation needs a new revolution."*
*(Thomas Jefferson)*

### MY STORY

My name is James Taris, and I am a LETSaholic. That is, I cannot get enough of LETS.

For those of you who do not know what LETS is, LETS stands for Local Exchange Trading System. It is a group of people from a small community who all agree to exchange goods and services with each other without the need for cash.

Once you have grasped the LETS philosophy, then trading in LETS points becomes an enjoyable and rewarding experience.

My LETS philosophy is ...

Do not think of LETS points like dollars. Think of them as favours. LETS Favours.

I became involved with LETS in 1993, and once I understood and accepted the principle of give-and-take with my fellow LETS members, I quickly noticed a sharp rise in the quality of my lifestyle.

Having a limited income meant I could only afford to pay for the essentials in my life: rent, gas, electricity, phone, petrol, food, clothes, and so on. Everything else became a luxury, which I either did without, or chose to do myself.

That all changed with LETS, because I found I could at last enjoy some of the luxuries in life by offering a range of goods and services through my LETS group. Very soon I was mowing lawns, removing rubbish and painting rooms. Later I was also designing business cards, brochures and newsletters; I even traded tiny picture frames, small bookcases and kitchenware.

In return I received massages, piano tuition and restaurant meals; computer support, computer software and web design services; greeting cards, teddy bears and bonsai plants. I would have reluctantly bypassed these goods and services if I had to pay cash for them. Thankfully, LETS made them all possible.

So how did I become a LETSaholic?

I was a wedding-portrait photographer for eighteen years, and in mid-1993 I decided I did not want to take photographs anymore, so I closed down my studio and found myself out of work.

I heard about this "LETS thing", where people could get goods and services without paying cash, so I found the nearest LETS group to my home, North Melbourne LETS (NM LETS), which was a twenty minute drive away, and I joined. When they asked me to list the things I could offer other LETS members, I chose commercial photography. After all, I was a professional photographer. Surely, I would be a great asset to their group.

After I paid my annual membership fee, which was only five dollars and five 'razoos' – a razoo was a NM LETS point – I was given a copy of the group's newsletter, The Brass Razoo, which also included their LETS skills directory. It was an orderly and detailed list of the goods and services offered by its members, and as I skimmed through the pages I saw dozens of items I was sure I could use: books, CDs and software; piano lessons, computer lessons and writing lessons; restaurant meals, bonsai plants and massages.

I was going to wait for someone to contact me first because I did not want to risk being rejected by any of the people I contacted. I was unsure how they would react if I asked them for something before I had actually done something for them first. I was more comfortable about earning some LETS points before spending them. I was sure that once the word got out about the professional quality of my photographs, I would soon become a popular choice with the LETS members.

So, I waited by the phone, waiting for it to ring; and I waited, and I waited. But the phone did not ring, and nobody came around. Even though the LETS group sent me their newsletter every three months inviting me to their LETS get-togethers – where I could meet other LETS members socially over a meal and drinks – I could not get over my fear of rejection, so I waited and waited some more.

Eleven months later! – on a Thursday night after nine o'clock – I was driving through North Melbourne where I knew there was a LETS get-together taking place. On the spur of the moment I decided to drop in, but just for ten minutes or so. I convinced myself that such a short visit would not be long enough to make me feel uncomfortable, and seeing it was already very late, I guessed the event would not be going on for much longer anyway.

The LETS Get Together was at the LETS office, and being a warm summer's night, the LETS members had congregated in the rear yard. I made my way through the office and as soon as I got to the back entrance, a short, stocky young guy – about twenty-three – came up to me and shook my hand.

"Hi, my name's Ross. If you want any heavy lifting done, any manual labour, digging gardens, moving house – that sort of thing – just call me and I will come and help you," and once he finished his introduction he just smiled at me and kept shaking my hand in anticipation.

It took only a couple of seconds for me to realise it was my turn to do some talking, so I said, "My name's James, and I am a photographer."

"A photographer!" he said excitedly. Then he started asking me about my occupation, and I immediately felt welcomed.

After a couple of minutes, he took me over to meet some of the other members.

"This is Doone who offers catering ... and this is Malcolm who offers labouring ... and this is Amy who offers sewing ..."

And Amy said, "If you've got any buttons missing from your shirts, or you want anything shortened or taken in, then call me and I will fix them for you."

So, in the space of just a few minutes, I already felt like one of the family. In fact, I was getting annoyed with myself for putting off meeting these people for so long.

There were not many people at the tables, so I asked Ross, "How come there is only seven people here tonight? I thought there were about eighty members in the group."

"This is only half the people who came tonight. But you are late – it is nearly half past nine and we started at half past six. Some of the members had to leave because they are working tomorrow morning, and others had to go home because they've got baby-sitters waiting for them."

I was curious about what the other members were offering, so Ross filled me in. "Now let us see … Peter was here, and he offers gardening … Bev offers ironing … Robert offers massage …"

"Massage!" I interrupted, "I'd love a massage!"

"Well", Ross said, "Robert's the best guy to give you a massage, because he runs massage classes. I am sure he'll do it for you if you ring him."

With that recommendation, I rang Robert the next day. Robert came over on the following Sunday and gave me the best massage I had ever had. Actually, it was the first massage I had ever had ... but it was fantastic.

All the while I could not help thinking that, there I was, unemployed, and enjoying a massage; a luxury I had never experienced while I was working because I could never justify paying sixty dollars to have it done. However, through LETS it had finally become a reality. That massage, my first LETS trade, made such a huge impact on me, it was as if I had been hit on the head with a sledgehammer. These people had shown me good old-fashioned help-thy-neighbour values, and it was contagious.

From now on, I thought, I would do whatever I could to help the LETS members get more of what they wanted. I had experienced how good it felt for someone to help me with my request and I wanted the other members to have that same wonderful feeling. I imagined the Domino Effect would then come into play and ensure everyone in the group became more active and helpful. That would impact on their lifestyles, making the group more effective and the members much happier.

In fact, I even thought about starting my own LETS group in Coburg, the suburb where I lived. I came to the conclusion that the lack of contacts from NM LETS members was probably due to the fact that I lived so far away from them. Whereas I had a car, many of the members had to travel by public transport. Indeed, I was very impressed that Robert rode his bicycle on the day he came and gave me that memorable massage!

However, after making enquiries at the Coburg City Council offices, I discovered there was already a LETS group near my home: Coburg and District LETS (C&D LETS) – which operated out of a Neighbourhood (Community) House only five minutes from my home. Within minutes I had joined that group as well and volunteered to help them with their newsletter. Even though C&D LETS had been operating for about a year it was still only a small LETS group with just 15 members. Up until then, they were only publishing a single-page newsletter, printed on both sides. I had seen how much more informative The Brass Razoo was, so I wanted to design a newsletter that was as good as that, or maybe even better!

But I had never designed a newsletter before, so I was unsure if C&D LETS would accept me. Fortunately, they were thrilled with my offer – it was not long before I realised that nobody else wanted to do it – and they also agreed to give me the training necessary to do the job properly. Soon I had my own desk space in their office and unlimited access to one of their computers.

The training and supervision were superb, and once I became familiar with the desktop publishing software, I completed my task without further supervision. The result of that caring and nurturing was the group's first twelve-page newsletter. I became so good at my newly acquired skill, that very soon, as well as producing the C&D LETS newsletter and directory, I redesigned all the group's literature and stationery: registration form, membership card, letterhead, leaflets, triple-fold brochure, and LETS transaction book. It was truly a labour of love and I eventually took up desktop publishing as a career; pleased to offload the stigma of being unemployed.

Over the first few months my involvement with C&D LETS continued harmoniously. Apart from producing the group's newsletter I also traded quite regularly with the LETS members. Having seen how willing the members were to offer their services to me, I added several more services to my list of Offers – lawn mowing, painting and rubbish removals – and rather than wait idly at home for the phone to ring, this time I took the initiative to contact the members myself. I gave and I gave, as a caring person gives, without thinking about what I would get in return. And yet, in return I got so much more than any other member in the group. Then as the group became more active, the membership also began to grow.

LETS also played a major part in helping me develop a range of new skills including desktop publishing, writing, administration, web design, public speaking and acting. So, all in all, these LETS experiences created a 'LETSaholic'. And if giving willingly of my time and skills to people who seek my help is regarded as addictive, then I am proud to be a LETSaholic.

I shudder each time I think back to my first year with LETS. I could still kick myself for waiting eleven months before making my first trade. What would have happened if I had not gone to my first LETS get-together? What would have happened if Ross had not encouraged me to phone Robert? What would have happened if I did not ring Robert? The answer is the same for all those questions and it still makes me feel sick. Just like tens of thousands of ex-LETS members around the world (thirty percent never ever trade!) I would have quit LETS at the end of my twelve-month membership, assuring myself that LETS was not such a good idea after all. The motivation that drove me to enlighten LETS members at every opportunity, was the incredible difference I felt between the ecstasy I experienced after my first LETS trade and the nausea that hit me when I realised I may have missed out on the LETS experience altogether.

Over the last ten years I have been involved with the administration of several LETS groups and been exposed to the operation of dozens of others. I am often asked, "What's the best way to run a LETS group?" and my answer has always been the same: "Do more of the things that encourage trading and less of the things that discourage trading."

That is what I did. I performed in many LETS committee roles over the years including Co-ordinating, Promotions, Membership, Newsletter, Directory, Web Site and Administration. In every case I focused on ways to increase trading amongst the members, being ever conscious of pursuing activities that made trading easier and avoiding activities that made trading more difficult. This has become my 'twist' – the LETSaholic Twist – on the original LETS concept.

LETS has been a wonderful discovery for me, and it has changed my life. This book gives you a detailed account of how I improved my lifestyle through LETS. I sincerely hope you will glean some useful ideas from the following chapters so LETS can do wonders for you too.

# CHAPTER 2

## LETS Favours

*"What do we live for if not to make life less difficult for each other?"*

*(George Eliot)*

## I SEE THE LIGHT

I had only produced the LETS newsletter for a couple of months when I noticed the account balance of one of our members was over a thousand LETS points in debit. That rang warning bells in my head. All the literature I had read about LETS warned of such situations and how 'the wealth of the local community' was being sapped by such members who took from the system without giving back.

With those thoughts in mind I rushed to the LETS co-ordinator to let her know my discovery.

"Sue, one of our LETS members is now over a thousand LETS points in debit. Do we have a debit limit? ... Do you want me to freeze her trading account?"

"Whose account is it, James?"

"It is Helen's. She's over twelve hundred points in debit now."

The next few minutes forever changed my outlook on LETS and had an unparalleled impact on me and my LETS life.

"Ah ... Helen. Let me tell you a little about Helen, James, but let me precede that with a small observation I have made. LETS attracts lots of different people, but they primarily fall into two groups: those who like to help people, and those who really need help. We have a small membership, and most of them are mature-aged. They are our best helpers because they are fairly comfortable with their lives, and if LETS did not exist, they would still be inclined to help others: it is typical of what their generation is used to doing. On the contrary, Helen is a single mother with an eight-year-old child and she recently purchased a house in Brunswick. It is an old run-down house with much need for renovating. These debits are a result of members helping to make her house more livable – turning it from a house into a home. Helen is the other half of the LETS equation: right now, she really needs our help."

Sue noticed I needed a little more persuasion, so she continued.

"Debit balances can be a real problem in a LETS group when it becomes apparent that a member is abusing the system by taking without any intention of giving back. Now let us take a look at Helen's offers. First of all, she has a piano, and although she does not teach piano lessons, she is offering the use of her piano for anyone who wants to take piano lessons in her home. Secondly, she is offering gardening, which is a high-demand service in our group. When she gets settled in her home, I am sure she will be pleased to help other LETS members improve their gardens. And finally, she is the only member we have who is offering holiday accommodation. She has a little country house near Ballarat that she is happy to make available to our LETS members for a couple of days or even a couple of weeks at a time. I have already been there myself, and it is a lovely place to go and just relax for a while. Helen is not a freeloader. She is currently a mother with a child who needs our help, and once she has settled in, you will see, she will become one of our most active traders."

Then Sue concluded with a revelation that I have since adopted as my own:

"James, LETS points are not dollars. They are more like favours. And when you can accept these LETS points as just being "favours" from one member to another, you will not be concerned about the balances on their accounts; either in debit or in credit. And really, what does it matter if Helen is not able to bring her account balance back to zero. I am sure most of our members, especially our helpers, will take pride in knowing they have helped one of 'us'. These members, you will notice, have credit balances – some quite high – and most have never asked other members for any help, and never intend to. They are Givers and do not really want anything back in return. They are just as excited about giving to our members, as those that are helped are excited about receiving. In their minds, they are simply doing favours for our LETS members, just as they would for their neighbours, families and friends."

From that moment on, I knew exactly what LETS was ... at least to Sue and to me and to our LETS members. That LETS philosophy has stayed with me for ten years and it is the key motivation that drives me to be such an active participant in 'all things LETS'.

My understanding of what Sue shared with me in such a caring way was that the LETS account balances were just a record of how much each member was giving to, or receiving from, the LETS group. It was necessary to keep record of each member's trading activity so they could then strive to bring their balances back to zero, thereby keeping the system as fair as possible for all.

By far, the biggest improvements I have seen in LETS groups have come about after members changed their concept of the group's purpose from that of being a local 'employment' or 'barter' system to that of being a 'self-help' group. Along with that comes a new understanding of what a LETS point really represents: changing it from being an alternative to cold, hard, 'cash' … to a much warmer, 'favour'.

## KEEPING SCORE ... NOTHING MORE

So, my LETS philosophy is ...

Do not think of LETS points like dollars. Think of them as favours. LETS Favours.

It was easy for me to accept this attitude because my first contact with LETS members, at the NM LETS Get-Together, presented them in the same way. They were offering their services to me without any hint of obligating me to give back to them. Then, when Robert cycled all the way to my home – maybe over an hour's ride! – and gave me a massage that lasted for two long and extremely relaxing hours, I felt he was doing it in the same caring way. I did not ask for a two-hour massage, but Robert noticed my muscles were very tight – due to stress – and needed additional massage, so he did what was best for me. And when I volunteered to design the newsletter for C&D LETS, whenever I was stumped and needed help, it was given to me at once and without hesitation.

I am very similar to most people so I am sure I would be hesitant to "give" if I felt the LETS members were trying to take advantage of me. It is human nature to treat people as they treat you, so when LETS members gave to me unselfishly, I gave back to them in the same way. This is the LETS attitude I tried to instill on every LETS member I came in contact with ever since.

So, what is a LETS point to me?

Let me start by saying that the generally accepted view by all LETS people is that a LETS point is not cash, or federal currency, and I agree. However, I do not feel comfortable viewing LETS points as an alternative currency with an equivalent value in cash. I prefer to interpret LETS points as being like LETS favours. That has always made trading more enjoyable for me. I love doing favours for members and they show genuine appreciation for the favour – in LETS points. It doesn't get any better than that!

I view LETS more like a voluntary self-help group where like-minded people in a local community give their time and experience to help their fellow members and feel welcomed to ask for the same in return ... just as they would from family and friends.

But rather than do all this helping without any recording at all, keeping LETS accounts allows the group to keep track of the members' activities so they can balance their trading activities fairly, knowing that once their accounts are back to zero, they have given to the group just as much as they have received. Basically, it is just a matter of keeping score and nothing more. This is how I like to explain LETS accounts to new members:

The LETS group's function is to act as a bookkeeper for their members' activities; keeping record of these 'favours' and putting the members' accounts into debit or credit accordingly. An account that is in credit identifies a member who has given more favours than he has received, and an account that is in debit identifies a member who has received more favours than he has given. These credits have no value and cannot be exchanged for cash. Their only purpose is to keep track of each member's involvement in the group so they can aim to bring their accounts back to zero — a sign of fair and equitable participation in the system.

The presentation I gave to LETS groups around the world was aptly titled ...

## LETS Favours:
### Improving your lifestyle through LETS

I noticed the biggest impact I had on an audience was when they grasped the LETS Favours concept. That mind-shift produced a couple of results I am very proud of: an immediate increase in membership – half the guests in the audience joined on the same night – and an increase in trading for the following month (usually about thirty percent). The type of feedback I received from audience members, especially from inactive members was, "I feel much happier about trading if I think I will be helping people". So, it seemed that members would rather trade when they thought of LETS points as 'favours' rather than 'money'.

I also found that focusing on helping members built a community-spirit within the group and placed a friendlier tone on each trade. That motivated me much more than being profit-motivated. As far as I was concerned, LETS points did not have any monetary value. They simply represented the value of appreciation shown by the member who had been assisted.

The LETS members I helped over the years knew I was not obligated to help them. Trading through LETS was never compulsory; it was always – and still is – optional. The members were grateful to get my help; in fact, any help. It was obvious just how appreciative they were because when I performed tiring services for members – such as lawn mowing, painting and rubbish removals – they always offered me snacks and drinks. They never even complained if my work was not 'spot on'. Why would they? Would you complain to your neighbour if he agreed to help you with some tedious chore? Would not you just be grateful that he agreed to be there and help you as best he could? That was how a community-spirit was built within the group. That was how trading became a friendlier and more enjoyable activity. And that was how I saw LETS: a voluntary self-help group of members who were willing to help each other in times of need.

Here is a detailed example of the caring and sharing that took place with my LETS hosts while I was travelling overseas ...

## IT IS ALL ABOUT CARING AND SHARING

In March 2004, Kit, my LETS host in Kitchener (Ontario, Canada) asked, "Can you paint a room for me?"

Now, you had to keep that request in perspective.

My stay in Kitchener was originally supposed to be for only one week: January 11-18. Nine-and-a-half weeks later, however, I was still there! Apart from a couple of weeks spent in Welland, Brantford, Montreal, Granby, Ottawa and Toronto, I spent the rest of my time in Kitchener ... and it looked like I would be there for another seven weeks, making it a total of over three months!

Now I was not in the habit of staying in the same place for such a long time; my average stay with a host was about a week. But things just turned out that way when my plans to visit South America fell through a couple of months earlier.

Not only that, but Kit also organised: two performances of my play, The Glory of Athens; three speaking engagements with local Toastmasters groups; a Murder-Mystery night; a winter camping weekend with thirty-seven other crazy Canadians; a visit to an Emu farm; a lift to Montreal, which was a six-hour drive; two lifts to Toronto and back (an hour each way); a cross-country skiing trip; and an ice-hockey game ... plus my day-to-day needs, as was originally requested when I first made contact with KW Barterworks, the LETS group Kit belonged to.

My commitment to the LETS group, and their commitment to me, ended after my first week, so all those extras had been provided by Kit.

When the visits to the South American countries had to be cancelled, Kit immediately offered to host me a while longer, because I was the ideal travel guest!

Here is why: I washed the dishes every day; I regularly shovelled snow from the paths and driveway around the house; I registered a domain name for Kit is business web site; I also provided the web hosting; I gave web page design tuition; and I was good company to have around, always having something positive to say.

The more I did for my host, the more my host did for me. It was all about caring and sharing, and having said that, I was not going to paint a room … I was going to paint the whole freakin' ground floor! That was four rooms and a staircase, which meant stripping paint off all the woodwork – doors, windows, skirting boards, and staircase; filling in cracks in the plaster; then painting the ceilings and floors.

Why would not I?

On my travels, there were many times when I had 'given more' or 'received more' than our original agreement had stipulated. To be quite honest, I found my hosts exceeded their obligations on almost every single occasion. Here are a few examples I recall from my European and African LETS Speaking Tour in 2002:

In England, I had use of a bicycle for a week and repaid the favour by doing a few hours of house renovating for another member.

Also, in England I cleaned a kitchen, bathroom and toilet. I got no extras in return, but I knew my host was expecting a visitor for the next couple of days, and because he was working all day, he would not have enough time to clean those rooms himself. So, I did it for him and when he got home, he could not believe his eyes!

In Spain, I washed the dishes one morning while my hosts were sleeping in. I just wanted to be helpful.

In Norway, I was given a Polynesian Massage and repaid the favour by helping out in a couple of ways before I left. *[details Chapter 3]*

In South Africa, I got my first taste of working my butt off for LETS. I was giving up to three LETS presentations each day for four days, and by the fifth day I lost my voice!

As you can see, we just helped each other out whenever possible. But I digress, so back to painting those four rooms for Kit …

When was the last time you stripped? ... paint, that is.

Well, I only allowed two days for paint stripping. Meanwhile, six days later I was still stripping!

I had a couple of agonising days sanding the woodwork to a neat finish. Why agonising? Because I did not use sandpaper; I used steel wool soaked in mineral turpentine. Very soon I found that applying pressure with my thumbs gave the best results. Unfortunately, it made them ache so much that I could not snap my fingers for six days! Just as well I was not performing my play during that period because when I played the role of Archimedes, snapping my fingers was an essential part of my act!

*[Details about my play, **The Glory of Athens**, can be found in my book, **From Fantasy to Hollywood**]*

What started out as a simple weekend paint job, turned out to be a self-inflicted sentence lasting about three weeks. The results, however, were very worthwhile and I never regretted it for a moment.

How did I go about my work? In a very organised fashion ... just like everything else I did.

Here is how long it took:
-one day of planning and re-organising four rooms;
-one day of emptying three rooms of all furniture;
-one day of removing a wallpaper strip, filling wall cracks and seventy-nine holes, repairing a door handle, removing loose plaster off the kitchen ceiling, buying paints and painting equipment;
-six days of stripping paint off the woodwork;
-two days of sanding;
-two days of painting;
-and one day of replacing furniture in rooms and stacking books and CDs back into shelves.

That completed three rooms of painting before I had to leave on my Ottawa LETS trip. However, on my return I completed the job by painting the kitchen as well.

That took another:
-two days of stripping paint;

-one day of filling cracks;

-one day of sanding;

-and two days of painting.

A grand total of twenty days!

But what a great job! I was very neat and considerate, cleaning up after myself at the end of each day. In fact, it was very reassuring to know that if I ever ran out of audiences to speak to, and web sites to design, I could always offer to renovate houses!

# CHAPTER 3

## Offers

*"The quality of your work, in the long run, is the deciding factor on how much your services are valued by the world."*
*(Orison Swett Marden)*

## WHAT SHOULD I OFFER?

When I joined my first LETS group, I did not know much about LETS. I was introduced to it some years earlier by one of my studio photographers who felt it would be an ideal way to generate more portrait sessions for my studio. Since then I lost contact with him and did not know anyone else involved with LETS. I was even approached by a representative from a commercial barter organisation who went into great detail on how my photography business would benefit if I provided photographic services to their members for 'trade dollars'. Therefore, I presumed that all these barter groups – and at the time I believed LETS to be a barter group as well – catered only for businesses. No wonder I chose to offer commercial photography to the LETS members. I did not want to take wedding and portrait photos anymore. I did, however, want to break into the commercial photography industry – a very competitive and specialised branch of photography that was almost impossible to get into. Anyway, commercial photography would be more appropriate because these were all businesses, right? Wrong! I did not realise the members were not businesses until after I joined and glanced through the LETS directory. I had not given any thought to offer anything else, and the girl taking my membership fee seemed happy enough with my Offer, so I let it stand.

I assumed that once I joined everything would automatically fall into place and I would soon become quite active in the group ... but that did not happen.

In hindsight, I made a very basic mistake: a mistake that could have been avoided.

## LIST OF SIX OFFERS

When I did not get any requests from NM LETS members for my commercial photography services, I should have realised it was not as popular as I thought. But until my first trade nearly a year later, I did not have the encouragement, or confidence, to correct the situation.

That all changed when I joined C&D LETS. To avoid falling in the same trap again, I immediately offered a much larger range of services. As it was my job to prepare the LETS directory each month, I took the opportunity to increase my list of Offers with every new issue; in fact, at one point I had a list of fifteen Offers. This did two things: it increased my chances of satisfying the needs of more LETS members; and it showed my eagerness to trade. I was always attracted to members who displayed a longer list of Offers. It made me more confident about contacting them because the message it sent out so blaringly was, I WANT TO TRADE!

There were only sixteen members in C&D LETS, so I recommended each member increase their list of Offers to at least six. It was simply a case of arithmetic: if everyone listed one Offer for exchange there would only be sixteen items being offered in the LETS directory; but if we all listed six items each there would be ninety-six!

## WORLD'S LARGEST LIST OF OFFERS

The following year, in 1995, when I co-founded Melbourne LETS with Bill McPherson, I took this idea to a previously unheard of level. A core group of only three people decided to start this new group. Bill had a list of four Offers: plumbing advice, business advice, computer advice, and computer hire; and Henk had a list of seven Offers: advertising consulting, marketing consulting, computer communications, computer hardware, computer repairs, computer software upgrades, and computer training. While this showed a keen willingness to participate by each member, it was hardly enough to encourage new members into the group; especially because their Offers were almost entirely business- and computer-related, and from experience I noticed that LETS members were very much non-business people.

I was determined to make the Melbourne LETS Directory much more user-friendly. It needed more Offerings, especially non-business goods and services. After consulting the NM and C&D and Brunswick LETS directories, I listed all the Offers I was capable of providing, ending up with a list of ninety-three Offers!

They included:

**ARTS & CRAFTS:** Banners (custom designed), Calendars (custom designed), Cartoonist, Framing, Greeting cards and invitations, Photographer (weddings/portraits), Photo restorations

**BUILDING TRADES:** Handyman, Labouring, Painting

**BUSINESS:** Advertising brochures/flyers, Business cards and letterheads, Business consultant, Business functions organised, Business planners (weekly/monthly), Certificates (designed to order), Copywriting for advertisements, Debt counselling, Delivery service, Distribution agent, Goal-setting (assistance with), Logo design, Marketing consultant, Motivational speaker, Name tags and name cards, Network marketing, Newsletter publishing, Office cleaning, Office organiser (chaos quelled), Office work/administration, Photographer (commercial), Presentation folder production,

Promotions adviser, Sales training, Time management, Training manual production, Trouble-shooter, Typesetting, Video production (corporate)

**COMPUTER:** Adobe Illustrator tuition, Adobe Photoshop tuition, Computer assistance, Computer operator, Corel Draw tuition, Desktop publishing, Microsoft Publisher tuition, Quark-XPress tuition

**DOMESTIC:** Budgeting (personal) - making ends meet, Car washing/detailing, Driver, Outings (organised & supervised), House cleaning, House minding (nights only), Household organiser (chaos quelled), Rubbish removed, Trees/hedges trimmed, Window cleaning

**EDUCATION:** Computer lessons, Driving lessons, Greek lessons, Maths tutor, Network marketing training, Photography course, Sales training, Song writing, Telemarketing tuition, Video production tuition

**EMPLOYMENT SKILLS:** Interview skills, Job applications

**ENTERTAINMENT:** After-party clean-ups, Cassette dubbing (audio), Party organising, Waiting (not just hanging around!)

**GARDEN:** Gardening, Lawn mowing, Trees removed

**HEALTH AND WELL-BEING:** Diet advice/support, Exercise advice/support, Lifestyle advice/support, Relationship advice/support, Stress management advice/support, Weight management advice/support

**MISCELLANEOUS:** Barter agent, Interpreter (Greek), Odd jobs, Research assistant, Sounding board

**SPORTS & RECREATION:** Chess partner, Golf partner, In-door cricket fill-in, Swimming instructor, Tennis partner

**TRAVEL & ACCOMMODATION:** Accommodation for travellers (upto 7 days), Tour guide, Office facilities - use of (upto 7 days), Photographer (special occasions), Travel companion.

Of course, I was not asked to perform all of these services. In fact, I only provided a few; but that was the whole point of the exercise. Except for lawn mowing, rubbish removal and painting, I learned it was virtually impossible to pick which services would be in greater demand. By having a longer list I was assured of becoming more active in one way or another. Apart from that, a longer list really impressed prospective LETS members who made comments such as, "You can learn how to speak Greek as well?" When I asked if they wanted to learn Greek, they would say, "No, but I am just impressed that someone could if they really wanted to."

Some members still cringe at the thought of making their lists longer. "If I add more items to my list, I will not have time to do anything else!" they say. That, however, is a huge misconception. A member who only offers carpentry or plumbing would certainly be run off his feet if he accepted every request; but he doesn't: no one does! Members can decide for themselves how many trades they accept through LETS. The point of this exercise was simply to make a list long enough to attract new members to our new LETS group and give them enough choices to make their first trade.

## LETS GRYN

An excellent example of how this worked for me was when I visited Norway on my Europe and Africa LETS tour in October 2002.

My LETS Favours presentation was featured in The Week in Aas Festival program, so it attracted many non-LETS guests to my talk. To make sure they understood how LETS worked, before I commenced my seminar, I shared some basic LETS information with them. I also thought it was a golden opportunity to earn some 'gryn' — Aas LETS points — to pay for the Polynesian massage I enjoyed the previous day. I also took the opportunity to show LETS members how easy it was to build a long list of Offers. That, I thought, would help counter the familiar but-I-do not-have-anything-to-offer argument.

So here is the list I came up with:

**CONSULTATIONS:** Dieting and Weight Management (I have lost seven kilos in the last five weeks), 4-4-40 Lifestyle Planner (how to work four hours a day, four days a week, for forty weeks a year), Self-promotion

**WRITING (also available internationally while in Australia):** Editing (and improving) Advertising Material or Business Letters, Editing (and improving) Short Stories and Poems

**ACTIVITIES:** Walking or jogging partner (if you hate exercising alone), Dance partner (I can also teach basic Rock 'n Roll), Taking photos (I was a professional Wedding and Portrait Photographer for eighteen years), Chess partner (I love playing chess), Cards partner (I can teach Con Can as well)

**LANGUAGES:** English Pronunciation (I have been living in Australia since 1956), Greek Pronunciation (I am Greek, and born in Greece)

**DISCUSSIONS:** Problem Solving, Brain Storming.

As you can imagine, the audience seemed quite amused by some of my Offers. In fact, I purposely included some things that would be unlikely to be requested. As I explained to them, "You never know what members will want, and anyway, there is no harm if you do not get requests for some of the things you offer."

Did I get to clear my debt to Aas LETS? You betcha! And just so you do not need to keep guessing, I was asked to be a 'dance partner' for a lady who was celebrating her birthday that night with fourteen other women. How lucky can a single guy get?

## TRY ME IN LONDON

I was introduced to one of the best Offers I have ever come across when I was in London on my 400-Day LETS Odyssey in 2003. I was invited to speak to the Camden LETS group. It was a cosy meeting in a member's apartment with maybe eight or ten members sitting on chairs and cushions in the lounge room. That night Phillida, our host, showed me their LETS newsletter and directory.

"One of our new members did not know what to list in her Offers because she was very versatile and could handle anything from secretarial work to house cleaning. She felt she would be happier to consider all requests made to her from LETS members. So, instead of making a lengthy but incomplete list, we came up with a new listing: 'Try Me'! It has since become very popular and now there are ten members listed in the Try Me category."

What a great idea, and very much in the spirit of LETS!

## CONQUERING THE FEAR OF REJECTION

The rejection I feared would happen – ever since my first day as a LETS member – never surfaced! Later I realised how lucky I was, because I heard many horror stories from members who were victims of it and either chose not to contact members anymore, or (unfortunately) became bad-publicity machines for LETS by complaining that "you can never get anyone to do anything for you in LETS".

My good fortune was that I volunteered to design the LETS newsletter, and I decided it should include the LETS directory. My fear of rejection still weighed heavily on my mind, so I contacted all the members in C&D LETS and made sure they were only offering goods and services they would be happy to supply. It just made good sense to me. There was nothing more frustrating than contacting members who did not want to (or could not) provide the goods and services they had listed on their list of Offers. Why would anyone offer something they were not going to do? Fortunately, after contacting all the members – remember there were only fifteen to call – I knew I had a SIZZLING HOT directory; and most of them were persuaded to increase their Offers to at least six goods and services.

I ensured the members were only offering goods and services they would be happy to provide by asking them to list: things they loved doing; skills they wanted to learn, improve or perfect; and items they did not want or need.

I felt this would create a more welcoming response to approaches from LETS members, as the only things being offered in the LETS directory now were for 'can-do' trades. Not only did the members agree it was a good idea, but they became very excited about contacting members in the future, now that their fear of being rejected had been removed.

## THE QUESTION OF CASH

Occasionally, I heard members say they preferred to earn cash rather than LETS points. Of course! So, did I ... but not through LETS! That was not what LETS was about. I always encouraged LETS members to make as much cash as they could ... outside of LETS. I considered members who asked for part payment in cash from LETS members, as taking advantage of the LETS system – even if they did not realise it. The effect of such trading, if it was allowed to continue, was to corrupt the whole system so that every other member saw LETS as an opportunity to earn more cash too.

My view was that in order to be truly effective, a LETS group would have to operate in a one hundred percent non-cash environment. That enabled cash-strapped members like me, to trade just by using their skills and without the need to supplement a LETS transaction with cash. The only exception to that was when a service involved the cost of materials. For example, when a handyman was asked to build a fence, the material costs would naturally be the responsibility of the member receiving the service. When I incurred a very small expense as a Giver – such as the cost of petrol for travel, or cost of ink for printing – I always preferred to ignore it rather than make an issue of it. It usually helped when I thought of what I would do if a neighbour, friend or family member asked for my help; I would never ask for petrol money but I would certainly ask them to buy the fencing timber.

There were two reasons why I thought LETS members should trade for one hundred percent LETS points and zero cash: it showed the Receiver that the Giver was trying to be helpful and not profit-motivated; and it enabled members with zero cash reserves to ask for those services, thus receiving the help needed to improve their lifestyles.

I always encouraged members to ask to be reimbursed for cash outlaid to cover the cost of purchasing materials required to carry out their service. In fact, I even suggested that the Receiver should purchase the materials himself; that would keep both Giver and Receiver honest: the Giver could not claim more than the actual cost outlaid, and the Receiver could not get away with not reimbursing the Giver.

## BUSINESS MEMBERS

I did not approve of businesses that wanted to sell their products through LETS and claim the wholesale cost of those products — in cash — from the Receiver. That, in itself, prevented cash-strapped members from trading with them. Nobody could verify what that cost really was — some businesses were asking for ninety-five percent of the trade amount in cash! — and since there was no real time spent in supplying a product, I felt that to be fair, the Giver should provide the product in lieu of the time not spent making the trade. Their gain – the difference between the amount received in LETS points, compared to their wholesale cost in cash — seemed, to me, to be an adequate reward, especially since most goods on the market were usually purchased at wholesale for only twenty to fifty percent of their retail price.

An acceptable alternative I offered was for those suppliers to act as purchase officers and order goods for our LETS members along with their normal wholesale orders. In that way they would be offering a genuine service to our members, and the wholesale cash price would then become the Receiver's

responsibility. After that, it was up to the Receiver to ensure —
through sighting a wholesale price list, invoice or receipt – that
the cash amount quoted was genuine. I was in business for over
twenty years, so I could see why my idea did not appeal to
some businesspeople who liked to keep their mark-ups private
... but I stuck to my point of view. I preferred to see our LETS
group go without getting access to some goods (a small loss to
our group) rather than have businesses come in and take 'cash'
advantage of our members (a huge problem for our group).

In my opinion, this was the best way for businesses to benefit
from LETS:

If a business wanted to increase its cash profits, it should first
make as much cash as possible OUSIDE of LETS. Then, if it could
not make any more cash, it should consider trading their
EXCESS GOODS AND SERVICES to our members FOR 100% LETS
POINTS. Thus, getting full value — in LETS POINTS — from
otherwise worthless goods and services. That way it benefited
both the business and our LETS members.

## MORE ON BUSINESS MEMBERS

After reading the above section on Business Members, I was contacted by LM, a LETS member, regarding my views on how business members should trade through LETS.

This was my response to his email:

*Subject heading:* **Businesses should only offer EGAFS through LETS**

LM: Although I have read similar statements, and it is the right of groups of people to trade in 100% CCs [community currencies], I do not see how it will help those most in need.

JT: I cannot see how it could do otherwise.

LM: It looks like a quick fix, but in reality, those that trade stuff that is more in demand in the money economy, will earn manymore points than they can spend, if they trade 100% CCs. The other option in such situations is that those participants in "high demand" will only trade with a "select few" participants and refuse CC trades to most others. That is my experience of what happens.

JT: Personally, I think it is silly for a business to offer their goods and services through LETS if they still have a [cash] market for them. They should only offer EGAFS ...

**EGAFS:** Excess Goods and Future Services

**Excess Goods** - products that can no longer be sold for cash or can no longer be sold at full price; **Future Services** - time or space that can no longer be sold for cash.

... then they will be happy to accept LETS points instead of cash.

I believe that businesses will join your LETS group, trade for 100% points, be happy, and stay forever ... but only if they are approached in the right way. This means that you have to let them know you want "what is best for their business" and NOT "what is best for your LETS group", even though this solution works out best for the LETS members too.

So here are the steps I suggest are taken ...

1 - Let them know that you want them to make as much CASH as they can, but not from your LETS group ... from the CASH community.

"Sell as many goods and services as you can, then when you cannot sell anymore, come to us and we'll buy - with LETS points - whatever you cannot sell for cash".

2 - Get them to value the goods and services available through your LETS group by showing them your LETS directory and making note of the items that can be of personal or business benefit.

"The LETS points you get from us can then be spent on any of the goods and services offered by our members in this directory. These will often be the little luxuries you would have 'gone without'."

3 - Reassure them that they will retain total control over what they offer for sale through your LETS group.

"And YOU tell us what goods and services you want to make available through LETS, and the terms and conditions under which you are willing to make the trade."

So, if it is a restaurant, their terms may be:

*Bookings essential.*

*Only valid from Monday to Thursday.*

*Maximum 6 LETS members per night.*

*Does not include seafood dishes or wine.*

*LETS members must arrive before 6pm (that gives him "bums on seats" so it helps to make his restaurant look popular).*

*That is how you get businesses to benefit from LETS: they reduce wastage (their EGAFS are still tradable); they increase their buying power (their LETS points can acquire lots of business and lifestyle goods and services).*

LM: Many naturopaths, and other service providers are technically taxable earning LETS points. Now, if they charge all LETS on their services, they will need to spend the points back on their business...

JT: This would be the second-best way for businesses to trade through LETS. [read on to find the best way!]

LM: ... or pay tax on them.

JT: This would be OK too. After all, they pay tax on cash earnings, so what's the problem? Of course, the amount of tax is always an unknown. Most businesses that NEED LETS, would be paying approximately NIL tax, so LETS would be an excellent way to help them improve their lifestyle. If they are paying a large amount of tax, I think they probably would not be interested in LETS ... unless they saw it as a way to make more cash in 50/50 trades. Then they become a profit-motivated member, and this tarnishes the LETS system. Eventually everyone they trade with feels they have a 'right' to charge 50/50 as well, even if they do not pay taxes.

Now for the best way for businesses to trade through LETS ...

My preference would be for the naturopath to offer non-business services through LETS. Then he would have no tax obligation on those trades. In fact, if he then spends his LETS points on business expenses, HE'S ENTITLED TO A TAX DEDUCTION ON THOSE TRADES! Now that is a completely different scenario, and I am sure if all tax-paying businesses adopted that strategy with LETS, then the tax department would very quickly lose all interest in recognising LETS points as being equivalent to cash.

LM: So, they either have to restrict the number of people they offer their services to, via LETS ...

JT: This is precisely what they SHOULD do. As per my restaurant example, the business should dictate how many trades they will accept each day, week, month or even year. Whatever suits THEM! They must see LETS as a benefit to off-load their EGAFS after they've exhausted all their avenues to sell them for cash. And a good LETS group co-ordinator should protect his group by not making it another avenue for businesses to make more cash sales ... whether they are profitable to a business or not. At the point where a business decides to trade through LETS, they should accept that their goods and services are worth NOTHING! (If they cannot be sold [for cash] then that is exactly what they ARE worth!) So, by trading them through LETS, WE

ARE DOING THEM A FAVOUR by accepting their goods and services in LETS points so they can then use them to fulfil their personal or business Wants. Shouldn't they be excited about that opportunity? I would! If I could turn goods and services worth nothing into my choice of hundreds of little luxuries offered through LETS, I'd be over the moon ... no matter what the tax scenario was.

Even if the tax was 50%, he would still be getting 100% of the value in LETS points, therefore still getting his Wants through LETS, effectively, at half price.

LM: ... or else find a way to earn 50/50 or other percentage and provide services to more LETS members.

JT: Sorry, the disadvantages of encouraging this far outweigh any possible advantages. The worst scenario is that it will kill your LETS group because many of the non-business members cannot obtain anything – even if they have thousands of LETS points – due to being cash poor. And if the group dies, the businesses will simply go on with their lives (remember, these were the ones in the 50% tax bracket that we thought we just had to have, and who justified asking for 50% cash to pay for their taxes!) while the people who really could've used LETS to improve their lives lose an excellent community-support group.

To be stable and ongoing, a LETS group should enable its members to trade without cash. That is the beauty of it. Once you allow part-cash trades in the system, you are really creating a system where members can buy DISCOUNTED goods and services. That is a completely different scenario and can only benefit members who have surplus cash. Or does it?

If a naturopath charges 50/50 for his trades and spends them on other services at 50/50, he'd be in exactly the same position as if he'd made the trades completely without cash. Or does he want to earn 50/50 and then only spend his LETS points on goods and services that do not ask for cash?

Is that really fair to the system and to its members? And how long do you think it'll be before the members all decide to ask for 50/50 trades as well?

Please do not take my views as being anti-business. I am actually pro-business in LETS, but in order to benefit BOTH the business and the LETS members, they should trade their EGAFS for 100% LETS POINTS. That is the only win-win scenario for everyone.

James Taris

www.LETS-Linkup.com

# CHAPTER 4

## Wants

*"Some desire is necessary to keep life in motion."*

*(Samuel Johnson)*

### NECESSITIES AND LUXURIES

When I first joined LETS, I thought I could get just about anything with LETS points rather than with cash. But until I made my first trade – eleven months after joining – I changed my thinking to the point where I thought I would be lucky to get anything at all with LETS points.

After that first massage, however, my hopes were raised again. Even if I could not get 'everything' with LETS points, maybe I could get 'enough to make a difference'; and that is exactly what happened.

Soon I divided my Wants into 2 categories: necessities and luxuries.

My 'necessities' included my basic living needs such as: rent, phone, gas, electricity, petrol, food and clothes. Even though occasionally there were fruit and vegetables available on the trading days, it was just a drop in the ocean as far as my food requirements were concerned. Realistically, all my necessities were still unavailable through LETS, and that was where all my income kept going. That killed any notion I had of saving money through LETS, my needs – my necessities – still had to be met with cash.

A whole new lifestyle opened up before me when I realised LETS could provide many luxuries. My 'luxuries' were the extras I learnt to live without or ended up doing myself. These extras could improve my lifestyle – if I had them or could get someone else to do them for me. Things like lawn mowing, gardening, painting, massage, computer tuition, piano lessons, gift items, books, etc.

That was why I became so excited after my first massage. It was the lift I needed to stop me feeling sorry for myself and help me see a brighter future ahead for my family and myself.

Here are several methods I used to track down my Wants ...

## FROM LETS SKILL DIRECTORY

I could never understand how some members would say they could not get ANYTHING through LETS. I could accept that I could not get EVERYTHING through LETS ... but ANYTHING?

Through the years, as soon as I received an updated copy of the group's LETS skills directory, the first thing I did was go through it, meticulously, and tick all the goods and services I thought I could use at some time. It was one of my greatest joys. Some of those items I went without because I could not afford them or could not justify spending cash on them. The other items I ticked were services I was currently doing by myself but did not enjoy doing.

If I could get other members to do them for me, it would free up my time and allow me to do things I really enjoyed for other members.

My mind was always on trading. I had earned lots of LETS points by helping many members, so using my LETS points to get little luxuries for myself was my reward. It was like winning a lottery and being given a catalogue of prizes to select from!

## FROM LETS MEMBERSHIP DIRECTORY

Using the LETS membership directory was very different from using the LETS skills directory. Rather than looking through the list of skills and seeing who could provide my Wants, I looked through the list of LETS members to see who I knew well enough to seek help for a specific Want. The contacts I made at LETS events and in the LETS office proved to be invaluable for that type of approach.

Going through the LETS membership directory was the method I used for one of my most requested Wants: moving house. Between 1999 and 2003 I shifted home address five times. Each time I moved without any stress at all. My house cleaners and packers, my trucks and trailers, my drivers and box carriers ... were always LETS members. They were affordable; I only used LETS points, and never had to pay any cash. They were reliable; they always turned up on time and with whatever tools necessary for the task at hand. And they were very caring; keen to make sure I did not have anything else for them to do before they left for the day.

I felt very comfortable calling these LETS members because they had already identified themselves as my friends.

# FROM LETS NEWSLETTER

As the membership in our LETS group grew, it became more and more difficult to include the LETS directory inside every newsletter issue. At some point the directory became a six-monthly production and the newsletter acted as an efficient monthly update. Hence, the LETS newsletter became another great source for satisfying my Wants:

**NEW MEMBER ADS:** My LETS newsletters were constantly introducing new members. Each new member was given a free Block Ad featuring his name, membership number, contact details and list of Offers. I liked trading with new members. From personal experience I knew how important a member's first trade was, so I endeavoured to meet new members and ask them for something: anything of use, really. Apart from seeing their excitement about getting into a LETS credit, I also liked the uplifting sensation I felt knowing I was getting things previously unavailable to me.

**KEEN TRADER ADS:** I also featured Keen Traders in my newsletters. They were members who made a special effort to promote their goods and services through newsletter advertisements. Obviously, they were keen to trade, so they became my first choice whenever I needed something done. That was especially important when I needed something done urgently. As a desktop publisher, my urgent needs usually revolved around getting computer help 'yesterday'. Occasionally my computer refused to do as it was told, so I sought the help of computer-literate members to repair computer hardware, reinstall programs, or tweak software programs back into operation. Apart from saving money (which I did not have) by not having to pay cash for professional computer help, keen traders also proved to be quick and efficient helpers.

**WANTED ADS:** Then, of course, if I could not find someone offering the goods or services I wanted, I placed my own ad in the newsletter's Wanted section. More often than not, a member would notice my ad and come to my rescue; though, I hasten to add, I noticed that my wanted ads were more successful than most. As I was well known by many of the members, and they knew I was one of the group's most active traders, I am sure they made a greater effort to help me; and quite often those were members I had previously traded with.

## FROM LETS TRADING DAYS

Whereas the LETS directory and newsletter were excellent ways to find the services I wanted, trading day events were my favourite way to find goods. As an avid reader and music lover, I collected many used books, CDs and cassettes from the trading-day stallholders.

I could not resist anything that came under the category of 'food and drink'. Trading days always attracted members offering jars of every conceivable type of jam, cakes, and even bowls of pumpkin soup. Fresh fruit and vegetables would occasionally show up as well, usually displayed – with pride – as being organic. Freshly baked bread was a rarity but just as popular, if not more so.

I could never understand how foodstuffs could be brought for trading and be allowed to be taken home because browsing members had opted to ignore them. I made a resolution to collect as much food as possible from these trading days rather than have them return home with the stallholders. Some of the foods had a long shelf life, and the perishables could either be eaten immediately or shared with family and friends. With that goal in mind, I developed the habit of turning up early to our trading days – as they say, the early bird catches the worm. However, I began to get a little self-conscious when some members would pass a stall and say, "Where have all the apples gone?" – or tomatoes, or bread, or jam (etc). It was time to rethink my strategy, so I changed it. When the trading day reached its peak, I announced, "If anyone's interested in Judy's jams, you would better come and grab some because I am about to take the lot!" I knew it was a cheeky thing to say, but it worked like a charm and the other members began getting their share of foodstuffs as well.

Those trading days were such a joy for me. At one pre-Christmas trading day I off-loaded almost one thousand LETS points on Christmas gifts. I got four handmade teddy bears (made from genuine kangaroo skin) for my children; at ninety points each they were exceptional value. Other items included an assortment of Christmas cards, bonsai plants and bicycle accessories. That day I also used my LETS points to get coffee and cakes.

I often observed members browsing through the LETS stalls. They would look closely at an item (say, a hand-made mug) then replace it and move on because the stallholder was asking ten LETS points for it. It was no wonder that many LETS members left those trading days without getting anything; they were relating LETS points to cahs! In Amsterdam, the Netherlands, Noppes – the largest LETS group in the world with nearly one thousand members – had the right idea about what a LETS point was. They called their LETS points, "noppes" – which means "nothings", in Dutch. I knew why LETS members at our trading days were rejecting LETS goods: they thought they could buy the same item for, maybe, half the price in cash. My attitude was ... I would prefer to part with ten 'nothings' (which equalled nothing) and keep my five dollars in my pocket (which saved me five bucks)!

# FROM LETS ONLINE TRADING

When I was in Canada, I came across a very successful way of LETS trading: online trading. It was being used by KW BarterWorks and one of their highest trading members, Pauline Finch (also a long-time board member and word-of-mouth promoter) did most of her trading that way; a habit resulting from an irregular schedule of graduate studies and part-time work that made it difficult for her and some other committed LETS members to get to as many 'live' trading day events as they wanted.

After talking to Pauline, I discovered she found 'new homes' for virtually everything she placed online within an average of forty-eight hours. In fact, when I last contacted her, her record was down to only six minutes, and her record number of respondents, for the same item within the first hour of electronic posting, was twenty-six! Pauline would also find many items for herself online and had acquired everything from curtain rods to a new kitten (!) using LETS points almost exclusively.

With over one hundred and fifty LETS members on their database, and several dozens of them active and regular online traders, it was no wonder the results were so good. When LETS members began asking how to post their Trading Offers online, Pauline came up with a basic guide to online trading. That guide, which she freely shared with me, was summarised in their seasonal newsletter, printed out for in-person distribution, and sent electronically (on request) to any member who asked for it. Members who traded online could also offer, in their text ads, to send digital photos directly to respondents who asked for them.

Pauline, who also traded more esoteric things – like classical sheet music and used musical instruments – on eBay, said that for local trading in small articles, or basic everyday services and supplies, "going online to LETS users is better by far, because it is personal and helps to grow the group right where we live. You already know the person at the other end of the email address, and they know you." I was so impressed, I introduced the online trading idea to Moreland LETS – my own LETS group back in Melbourne – and, after adopting it, they have since had great success as well. The following benefits of online trading were taken from Pauline's excellent Online Trading document:

**Online Trading – it is easy and effective**

Why Trade Online?

1. You reach everyone on the LETS e-group list simultaneously with one sending.

2. It is fair – every e-respondent's message contains a transmission time, so first-come can be first-served.

3. Potentially expands your LETS network to include new people you have never traded with before.

4. It saves time, overhead and energy.

5. It creates potential new customers for in-person events such as our monthly Trading Days.

6. Online trading makes trading from home easier for those without cars or easy mobility.

7. It is an ideal trading outlet for busy people who want to stay in the LETS 'loop' and earn LETS points regularly.

8. It is fun – you never know what will come up next, or who will have that elusive item you have always wanted.

*[This article was kindly submitted by Pauline Finch, of KW BartwerWorks in Kitchener-Waterloo, Ontario, Canada]*

# CHAPTER 5

## Trading

*"My trade and art is to live."*

*(Michel de Montaigne)*

## LIFESTYLES IMPROVE WITH EVERY TRADE

The best way I found to run a LETS group was to do more of the things that encouraged trading and less of the things that discouraged trading. In fact, while I was on tour and speaking to LETS members around the world, I told my audiences ...

"If no one is trading in your LETS group, you may as well close it down and throw away the key because it is not helping anyone. Or if it is only being kept active and alive for social reasons, then call it a Social Club ... but do not call it LETS!"

When I was involved in a committee role with LETS, my emphasis was always on increasing trading. I knew that was the only way to impact on members' lives. In my first year with NM LETS, my lifestyle did not change at all in the first eleven months – when I did not trade – so 'not trading' just kept the status quo. The only changes occurred after I made a trade; my lifestyle improved, or the lifestyle of another member improved because of my help.

I noticed that by increasing the trading activity in our LETS group, the group became stronger and more effective, thus building the confidence of the existing members and attracting new members to the group.

Once I began actively trading through LETS, I noticed how much more comfortable I was about trading with members I had already met. I was always confident about asking for help from a member I had already met. It was like phoning a friend; there was not any awkwardness like that associated with phoning a stranger. That was emphasised even more when I contacted members I had previously helped. After all, it was only after going to a LETS get-together that I got the confidence to make my first approach for a LETS trade.

Once I joined C&D LETS I placed a high priority on attending the monthly LETS events so I could meet other members and get to know them better. I found that attending those LETS events was the perfect way to build friendships and future trading partners. Likewise, when the other members got to know me, they were more comfortable about contacting me for help.

## FREQUENCY OF EVENTS

I could never understand why a LETS group would choose to hold fewer LETS events because of poor attendances. Any future events usually attracted the same poor attendances and, because there were fewer events, gave members fewer opportunities to meet and get acquainted with each other. Personally, I was never concerned about low attendances at LETS events. I remember going to a LETS event once where only three members turned up, and I was one of them! The outcome of that event was that all of us got to know each other extremely well and by the time we left we had all made appointments to trade with each other the following week. My newsletter report for that LETS event highlighted all the positives we had experienced on that day, and encouraged the other members to make sure they came to the next LETS event so they did not 'miss out' again next time.

My observation was that members lost interest, and confidence, in their group when LETS events took place at intervals longer than one month apart. Whereas holding LETS events more often than once a month became too overwhelming for members and caused lower attendances. There was one best time span between LETS events: monthly!

## TYPES OF EVENTS

On my globetrotting travels I came across many types of regular events organised by LETS groups. They included: LETS get-togethers, LETS trading days, LETS auctions and LETS Hit Squads. There was no 'best' type of event, but there was a 'best' way of organising them. The best results for those events was 'achieved when a committee member was responsible for organising it rather than just relying on a newsletter article to do the job. The organising always involved contacting members personally and asking them to participate in whatever capacity was required to make the event successful.

## LETS GET-TOGETHERS

LETS get-togethers are purely social events, where members and their families can meet for breakfast, lunch or dinner at the LETS office or in a member's home. Usually the members are asked to bring food and drinks to share. This type of event is also referred to as a LETS pot-luck dinner. The purpose of these events is simply for members to mingle and get to know each other.

Whenever I organised a LETS event for a small group of under one hundred members I found that LETS get-togethers were the most successful. Getting ten to twenty percent of members to attend our events was usually regarded as being normal, so it was more appropriate for a handful of members to get together over some food and drink and just chat in a social atmosphere. LETS get-togethers proved even more successful when a committee member greeted all members, especially new members, as they arrived … just as Ross had greeted me at my first LETS get-together. Whenever I got to these events – and I did not like to miss any – I made it a point to talk to every member I had not met before. I would approach the member with a smile and introduce myself:

"Hi, my name's James. And yours? ..."

"My name's Chris".

"Pleased to meet you, Chris. If you ever need any desktop publishing done ... things like business cards, brochures, advertising flyers, gift certificates – that sort of thing – just give me a call. Here is my business card. Do you think you might need anything like that?"

If they had ever thought about getting something designed and printed, they always told me.

"Well, whenever you are ready, give me a call and we'll make an appointment for you to come and get the work done. Those jobs only take an hour or two to complete, so I could design and print them for you while you waited."

That was really all they wanted to hear. Occasionally we would make an appointment on the same day, but it was more common for them to follow-up with a phone call some weeks or even months later: they always remembered my willingness to help.

The other half of the conversation was where I found out about them:

"So, what are you offering through LETS? ..."

Yes, Ross taught me well!

Some of my best trades were arranged through such friendly meetings. Even when we did not have anything of interest to offer each other, we still made a friendly acquaintance. However, because we then knew what we were both offering, we would occasionally recommend each other to members who showed an interest for our services. There was everything to gain and nothing to lose by meeting new members and simplifying trading between ourselves. That was when lifestyles improved. That was when lives changed.

## LETS TRADING DAYS

LETS trading days are trading events where members can trade goods for LETS points. It is not compulsory, however, to bring anything to trade. Actually, a successful trading day requires more browsing members than stallholders. The purpose of this event is to provide an environment where members can earn credits by exchanging their goods for LETS points and browsing members can use their LETS points to acquire goods through LETS.

When our group had well over a hundred members (usually over 150), then LETS trading days were our preferred type of event. In fact, whenever anyone enquired about becoming a LETS member, the LETS office made a habit of inviting them to our monthly LETS trading day. It was an excellent recruiting atmosphere and just about all those visitors became members while they were at the event.

I came across an excellent adaptation of the trading day while I was touring New Zealand in April 2003. I heard about LETS groups in South Australia inviting the general public to their trading days, but I never saw how it worked. On this day, I was fortunate to witness the most amazing LETS trading day in all my LETS years. It was organised by Helen Dew in Carteton, near Wellington, New Zealand.

Helen was hosting me for several days, and one of the first things I noticed when I arrived at her home were a bunch of neatly dressed dolls.

"These dolls," she said as she showed me five new dolls laid out on a tabletop, "were old dolls I'd found with damaged clothing. I gave them to one of our Green Dollar members who has washed their hair, cleaned their faces and made a new set of clothes and shoes for them. Now I can sell them at my garage sale."

Helen Dew was the Queen of LETS retail sales. Her volume of sales in Wairarapa Green Dollar Exchange was more than three times as much as her nearest rival. In fact, her exploits had received such wide recognition that she had been invited to speak at an International Money Symposium being held in Germany in July 2003.

How could Helen afford to travel to Germany for such a notable occasion? Simple. She held a fundraising Monster Garage Sale and coincided it with the usual LETS trading day. Here is a glimpse of how it all went …

Helen personally contacted all the LETS stallholders who were due to arrive at the hall at eight thirty, on the Saturday morning. Even though the market hall was just two blocks away, Helen was out the door by seven o'clock. The hall was on the main road through Carterton, so any traffic coming in or out of town was bound to notice it. As well as that, Friday's newspaper featured these four advertisements promoting the garage sale and my LETS presentation:

**Wairarapa WHAT IS ON section:**

SATURDAY, APRIL 5 … Green Dollar Exchange - Market/Garage Sale/Auction, St Mary's hall, corner High and King streets, Carterton, 9.30am – noon, a fundraiser for Helen Dew's conference in Germany. Contact Ruth C 123-5678.

***

Public Presentation – at 1pm, hear James Taris tell how he has used green dollars touring eight countries and in Australia. Contact Helen Dew 123-7654

## Wairarapa GARAGE SALE section:

GARAGE sale Market/Garage Sale/Auction, St.Marys Hall, cnr High and King streets, Carterton, Sat 5th April 9.30am - 12 noon.

\*\*\*

GARAGE sale monster auction market, St.Marys hall cnr High and King streets, Carterton, Sat 5th April 9.30am - 12 noon. Enquiries ph Ruth 123-5678.

\*\*\*

Two bright yellow sandwich boards were displayed outside the church hall for the previous three days. One simply wrote, 'MARKET', and the other one wrote, 'Saturday, April 5, 9.30am - 12.00'.

The other stallholders arrived after eight o'clock ... and there were lots of them, with lots of products. Why such a good response? Because these traders were going to sell their products to LETS members for Green Dollars, and to the public for cash! Not a bad incentive for stallholders to turn up.

A few stalls were set up inside the hall alongside Helen's stall, but because the weather was so fine, Helen encouraged most traders to set up their stalls outside the church, virtually on the street. That proved to be a great visual crowd stopper, and by a quarter to ten the traders were inundated with buyers. All the commotion died down by half past eleven, but Helen had not finished yet. She was about to off-load almost all her unsold goods by auction.

The auctioneer arrived just before noon and within an hour had cleared all her unwanted items, much of it purchased by the remaining LETS traders for unbelievably cheap prices, as low as one dollar per box of goods. Not a bad result for a one-morning fundraiser.

## LETS AUCTIONS

LETS auctions are also trading events where members can pick up goods for LETS points. These goods are supplied by members, and the total amount – in LETS points – bid by a member at auction is retained by the owner of the item. Apart from the use of LETS points, everything else is run like a normal auction. To be successful, a LETS auction must have large numbers of bidders in the audience – as not everyone bids on everything – so this type of event is best suited to groups with well over a hundred members.

If you have never had a LETS auction in your group, I can strongly recommend it. Members are asked to bring things from home to be auctioned for LETS points. Some of the more valuable items have a reserve amount that needs to be met before a bid is finally accepted, but most of the items have no reserve at all and are given for whatever bid can be obtained. This is a great way for members to clear out unwanted items from their homes, and it is an excellent way for members to pick up unbelievable bargains without paying any cash. When the event includes food and drink supplied by members, it becomes a very enjoyable social evening as well.

When I was in Wales in November 2003, I was fortunate to be invited to a LETS auction held by my hosting group, South Poweys LETS. Without any advance warning, I was asked to be LETS auctioneer. I had never done this before, but I was keen to try. John Rogers, the group's regular auctioneer, started it off superbly, and he was soon checking to see if I still wanted to try it. I sure did.

I started off hesitantly but finished with a bang! Seeing I got a few laughs and sold nearly everything, I guess I did pretty well for a beginner.

## LETS HIT SQUADS

LETS Hit Squads are 'working bees' that are organised for a specific task. This can be for the benefit of your LETS group or a LETS member, and all participants earn LETS points for their time. Hit Squads can be effective even with groups of less than a hundred members. They do, however, need to be organised by an appointed committee member, or broker, to find enough members to perform the set task (usually about a team of eight).

In September 2003, I stumbled upon the North Fife LETS (NFL) Hit Squad and was awestruck by one of the best ideas I have ever seen. Phil Beaumont, co-ordinator of North Fife LETS, borrowed the idea from a TV show.

"The Hit Squad in this show goes to a person's house and transforms it all in one day, while the owner's away," he said. "So, I thought we could do the same thing in our LETS group."

In the last 12 months the NFL Hit Squad had been a 'big hit' with their group, completing twenty-two projects including thirteen gardening, six catering and three decorating projects.

The secret to this success was their Hit Squad Co-ordinator (HSC). Obviously, every project required a different type of expertise, so it was the HSC's job to ring around and find a suitable team for the task. The HSC was awarded LETS points for her efforts, and rightfully so.

I never got to see them in action, but the image I had was of a team of members dressed in black with LETS HIT SQUAD emblazoned across their chests. Maybe green would be a more appropriate colour, but either way I am sure it would attract a lot of attention, and possibly be an ideal recruiting tool as well.

North Fife LETS had one of the most positive attitudes I came across on my travels, so it was no surprise that their small group of only eighty-seven active members had such great results with their Hit Squad. They were such an inspiration.

I came across a similar idea in August 2002, when it was introduced to me as the LETS Work Group concept. I was being hosted by BEETS in Bristol, England. Their original concept developed from a desire to form a Decorating Group, where LETS members met, more or less, on a monthly basis to help decorate the home of one of their members. Apart from the obvious benefit the homeowner enjoyed, there was the added benefit of 'bonding', where all the participants became better acquainted, therefore building friendships that were invaluable in any LETS environment.

Up until that time, the Work Group had successfully completed a variety of projects, including: decorating a front and back room; painting a hallway; knocking down a wall and cleaning the bricks; and building a garden shed.

# CHAPTER 6

## Administration Help

*"If there is no one there to help, go out and find someone to help."*

*(Bushido)*

## I HELP TO RUN OUR LETS GROUP

Shortly after I first joined LETS, I received my first newsletter from NM LETS – August 1993. It had a short advertisement on the back page:

PRIVATISED NEWSLETTER – Tenders are invited for production of the next four editions of the Brass Razoo. Interested members should submit a brief resume and a production cost (labour only) to produce 4 editions P.A. The successful tender will be given access to word-processing and photocopying equipment.

I wished I could produce their newsletter, but I had no experience with designing newsletters, and I could not submit a tender that, because of my inexperience, would be taken seriously. A year later, however, when I discovered C&D LETS, it was that same ad that motivated me to offer my services to them as a newsletter designer, even though I was not a member yet.

My introduction and involvement with both groups was very different: with NM LETS I was an orphan-member – I did not know anyone in the group – and I did not make my first trade until eleven months later; but with C&D LETS, I went straight into an administrative role and began trading immediately.

Even though at the start I was not getting any LETS points for producing the newsletter, I was very grateful to be learning a new skill and accepted that I was being adequately compensated by getting free desktop publishing training, use of their computer, and access to the office at any time during working hours.

I knew my help was being appreciated, so I redesigned all their LETS literature and stationery as well. Soon a stack of my newly designed LETS brochures was placed on the front counter, and whenever people with financial difficulties came to the Neighbourhood House, they were handed a LETS brochure. In that way we recruited a steady stream of new members.

Whereas NM LETS was a well-established LETS group, C&D LETS was a group still in its early stages of development. I saw many opportunities for me to grow along with the group. I realised that helping out in the LETS office was also a great way for new members to get acquainted with LETS. In many ways I gained through my involvement in the LETS office, and I knew that new members could get those same benefits as well. By offering to help C&D LETS in a role that interested me (LETS groups are always in need of help) they treated me like royalty.

These are the ways I benefited from taking on various administrative roles with LETS:

I increased the credit on my account by earning LETS points for my administrative activities;

I quickly learnt more about LETS and how it worked;

I learnt skills I did not have before, such as desktop publishing and web design;

and I met more members, more quickly, which led to more trading with them.

## EARNING LETS POINTS

Getting members to help with LETS administration always seemed to be a problem with LETS groups, so I suggested we reward their efforts by giving them ten LETS points per hour (our basic hourly rate) for each hour they contributed to the running of our LETS group. After all, these were not cash payments, they were just 'thank yous' – a way that our group could show their appreciation for the help received. Very soon we had ten administration, or committee, roles filled, and the group was running like clockwork. That system was also adopted by other LETS groups I joined and proved to be extremely effective.

A side-benefit to this new administrative decision was that we could recruit new members straight into an administrative role (just as I had done) with the promise of helping their LETS account go straight into credit. That was an ideal scenario for two types of new members: those who hated getting into debit, and those who were offering low-demand services.

Occasionally, I was surprised by a new member who refused my offer to help them satisfy their most urgent Wants. These new members, when they joined, insisted they wanted to get into credit first.

Initially it bothered me because I had visions of them sitting by their phone for months on end, just as I had done. Then I realised that some people were really scared of getting into debit, even though it was only in LETS points. My experience showed me that most new members needed to get something from the LETS group before they were confident that the system really worked and that we were not just trying to take advantage of them. But others, just a small minority, needed to earn credits before they got the same confidence.

Their fear was that they may get into debt, small or large, and not be able to clear it. And no matter how much time I spent trying to convince them it was not like a money system and we were not going to send debt collectors after them, they stuck to their guns and refused to budge on their decision. Finally, I became resigned to the fact that there were two types of new members and whether their first trade took them into a debit or credit, either trade was fine. It was crucial that I allowed the new members to trade in the role they were most comfortable with: Giver or Receiver. My solution to that dilemma was to help them make their first trade as a Giver. This is how I encouraged them to make their first trade:

"There are a few ways you can get into credit. First of all, you can wait for a LETS member to call you, but that can often take a long time – I did not get my first call for over a year! Or you can bring something to trade at our next trading day, which is on Sunday-week. Then, of course, you may like to help us in the LETS office. We could roster you on for a four-hour block and you would get ten LETS points per hour for your time. That is forty points per shift. They are the three ways you can earn some points. Which one would you like to try first?"

After that, I accepted whatever decision they made. I was just trying to be helpful. Anymore 'pushing' would probably turn them off LETS entirely.

Some members were convinced they did not have anything to offer; or were only willing to commit to offering just one obscure product or service without much prospect of any members ever contacting them for a trade. It was surprising how happy they were to come into the office once a month and help prepare the newsletters or directories. All of a sudden, photocopying, stapling, folding and licking postage stamps was a pleasurable way to earn a steady stream of LETS points. Of course, once they had helped in that way, it was quite common to see them volunteer to take on additional four-hour shifts during the month.

As members felt more comfortable helping in the office, they became excellent prospects for taking on a specialised committee role whenever one became vacant. There were many roles that needed to be filled in order to run a successful LETS group, and whenever I encouraged members to take on a LETS committee role, I recommended they only volunteer to perform a role that they would enjoy.

## LEARNING ABOUT LETS

LETS is not complicated, it is more of a mind-shift. It took me over a year to really understand it, but that was because I had no LETS interaction for eleven months. However, once I was welcomed into the C&D LETS office, I grasped the LETS concept within days. By soaking myself in LETS, I finally 'got it'.

Many aspects of LETS then fell into place very quickly for me. Once we received a LETS transaction in the mail, I followed its path to see how each of the trading members' accounts was altered; the Giver received a credit and the Receiver got a debit. Looking at the state of each members' accounts was also revealing. I was surprised to see that a member could have the highest credit in our LETS group without being our most active trader. That situation occurred when a member earned LETS points through trading but did not use those points by requesting anything from other members. In actual fact, our most active members were often alternatively in credit or debit as they frequently traded 'both ways'. They did lots of things for our members but were equally as busy asking other members to help them in return. A common term used by LETS people is "bringing your account back to zero". That was the ideal scenario sought by LETS groups from each member, where the members 'gave' to the system to the same extent that they 'received'. It was an excellent target to strive for.

Of course, everyone had their own ideas and opinions, so it was good to discuss them with other LETS members in the office. My biggest LETS lesson was learning that LETS points were really like 'thank yous' or 'favours'.

## DEVELOPING NEW SKILLS

I am eternally grateful to LETS for helping me develop skills that I dearly wanted to learn. Most of those skills were learnt when I became involved in various administrative, or committee, roles with a number of LETS groups.

I was interested in desktop publishing for several years, but it only became possible when I volunteered for the newsletter designer role with C&D LETS. Any earlier thoughts at learning desktop publishing 'in the real world' were deterred by huge tuition fees of between one and two thousand dollars. Not only that, but it was unlikely that a business risk teaching me those skills because workplace laws prevented that from happening unless they employed me. LETS, however, was able to do both; it gave me the desktop publishing training I needed and also allowed me to practise my skills on their group's newsletter. Wow, what a fantastic organisation!

Fortunately, I also had to write the articles for the LETS newsletter. I had been writing since I was twelve, but it was through my newsletter articles that my writing improved. I had always thought about writing books, but I could never get myself to start on a subject and stick with it. Writing articles for the newsletter proved to be a great breakthrough for me. Eventually I realised why I became more prolific with my writing. If you are a closet writer, as I was for many years, you may appreciate the writing revelation I had: you will begin writing once you know you have an audience.

The LETS newsletter was the vehicle I needed to commit myself to constantly producing articles for my LETS audience … and I relished it. That was way back in 1994.

Then in 2000 I had an urge to branch out into web page design, and even though I tried desperately for fourteen months to build my web design skills on my own, it was not until I accepted the role of Website Webmaster for my LETS group that it all finally fell into place for me … in just fourteen days!

My web sites became an ideal way to express myself. Now my audience had grown from an initial fifteen LETS members to a potential of millions of online Internet users!

## MEETING MEMBERS

A huge bonus for helping out in the C&D LETS office was that I got to meet all the members very quickly. For eleven months, I did not know anyone at NM LETS, hence my reluctance to contact anyone. It was such a joy to meet and talk with C&D LETS members, and because I was already helping them with the newsletter, I felt I was doing my bit for the group. That gave me the confidence to ask members to trade with me whenever I found they were offering something I could use.

Just seeing the LETS transactions that came through the office was inspiring. When I saw that James N was giving clarinet lessons to a member's daughter, I contacted him to ask if he would teach my daughter as well ... and he agreed! Then, because of that contact, I asked his wife, Lynette, to give my daughter piano lessons too. We developed quite a good friendship and I still remember helping them solve a couple of big problems.

James N told me he received a letter from the city council because the grass on the nature strip in front of his house was too long and was therefore regarded as a fire hazard – it was about two foot (sixty centimetres) high! If he did not cut it within fourteen days, they would send their own worker to do it and forward the bill to him. James N did not have a lawn mower … or excess cash, so he was really worried. Fortunately, it was a simple task for me, and I think his lawn was the first lawn I mowed for C&D LETS. Then, around Christmas time, I got another call from James N:

"Can you paint a few rooms for me? Lynette and the kids have gone to spend Christmas and New Year with her parents and I really want to get the painting done while the house is empty."

What happened after that was something I am sure James N still talks about to this day. Early in the morning, at seven o'clock on January 2, Peter – father of James N's other clarinet student – and I arrived at his home and within two days we painted four rooms with two coats of paint …and it was a damn good job, even if I do say so myself. James N was a great musician, but he did not know one end of a paintbrush from another.

Those two days are some of the best LETS days I can remember. There we were, Peter and I, helping out a fellow member in a time of need. James N bought all the materials we needed and kept us well fed and watered — he was a good cook. As he explained later, "LETS is fantastic. There is no way I could have got anyone else to come and help me just one day after New Year's Day. Everyone was on holidays!"

All that became possible because I made contact with James N while contacting all the C&D LETS members to update their LETS directory listings. He told me about his URGENT painting need, so I called Peter. Even though painting was not one of his Offers, he was happy to help a member who was already helping him with his daughter's music needs.

Those were the types of trades that became much easier when I was helping to run our LETS group.

# CHAPTER 7

## Rebuilding

*"Whatever good things we build end up building us."*

*(Jim Rohn)*

## LETS DO OR DIE

I noticed that whenever a LETS group had a slump in trading and membership, it was often an indication that confidence in that group had waned. At that point the LETS group would either; treat it as a warning signal and do something to increase trading, thereby restoring confidence in the system; or accept it as the death knell for the group and let it die. Unfortunately, the latter scenario was all too often the situation.

Whenever I was asked to help rebuild members' confidence in a LETS group, I found the best solution was to get the members trading again by helping them to get what they wanted through LETS!

My recommendation was to get the group's most excited or persuasive committee member to call everyone in the group and:

-explain that they wanted to do whatever they could to help the members get whatever they wanted through the LETS group;

-confirm that the members were still willing to offer the items on their list of Offers, and help them build their list up to six listings;

-ask the members to select items from a long list of goods and services that they could use "now or sometime in the future";

-and use that knowledge to arrange trades between the group's members.

By the time a LETS group reached such a critical stage, it had often lost many members — usually being left with only fifty members, or less, and maybe only half a dozen of those trading. So, doing the 'ring-around' would not take much time.

Depending on the size of the group, it was usually achievable within a few days, which was not long considering it most probably would save the life of the LETS group. It was also not an ongoing role either. Once the members started trading again, the confidence they had lost would be restored, and soon they would be making their own calls again.

# I CONTACT ALL MEMBERS

When I was designing my first newsletter for C&D LETS, I wanted to include the LETS Directory in it as well. As a new member, I was also keen to find out what was being offered by the other members. They did not have a LETS directory, as such, and I knew that more trading would take place when the members saw what goods and services were available through the group. With only 16 members in the group, I felt that an increase in trading would create the positive energy required to attract additional members – the only way, I thought, to sustain a LETS group for the long-term.

*[Note: On my travels I noticed that, on average, LETS groups had about one hundred members. Groups with under one hundred members were rather unstable, as members found it difficult to have many of their needs met and soon lost confidence in the system. However, when a group had about two hundred members it became very stable and members felt much more confident with the system that usually offered about one thousand goods and services in their LETS directory.]*

When I joined C&D LETS, the membership was more or less the same as when the group was first formed about a year earlier. I was still excited about how great I felt after my massage through NM LETS and I wanted to help C&D LETS become as big as that group, therefore making it as effective with their members' needs.

As a new member, I wanted get support for my idea, so I talked to Sue, our LETS co-ordinator, who agreed it was a good idea. Soon I had a phone on my desk and a C&D LETS Membership List.

It was still too soon to make any calls. I had to make sure I covered everything as best as possible, so I wrote a Member Contact phone script. It was quite lengthy, but once I got into it, the time passed very quickly, and the members did not mind the 'inconvenience'. In fact, the response I got after each call was very encouraging.

It went something like this:

Hi! Can I please speak to ... (Keith)?

*["This is Keith."]*

... (Keith!) My name's James Taris and I am a new member with Coburg and District LETS. I am calling from the LETS office where I am currently preparing the next LETS newsletter. In fact, I want to include an up-to-date LETS directory with the next issue. That is why I am calling you and the rest of the LETS members.

Do you have a few minutes to spare?

*["Sure"]*

Basically, I want to do whatever I can to help our members get more of the things they'd like through LETS, and one of the first things I want to do is clean up the LETS directory so it only contains goods and services that members are still willing to provide.

Do you mind if I ask you about your Offers and Wants?

*["Not at all. What do you want to know?"]*

First of all, I'd like to confirm that you are still willing to offer the items you listed on your list of Offers when you joined. You are down for ... (bicycle repairs and gardening). Can you still provide those services ... (Keith)?

*["I guess so."]*

Actually, I am asking all the members to only offer services they would really enjoy doing. That makes sure that whenever you contact another member, you will not have to worry about them saying, "No".

So, are you happy to provide ... (both bicycle repairs and gardening)?

*["Well, I am always working on my own bicycle, so I'd enjoy doing that for LETS members as well, but I am not so keen on gardening anymore, especially if they are big jobs. So maybe you can cross that one off."]*

Okay. Now, seeing there is only sixteen members in our group, we're not going to have much of a directory if everyone's only offering one thing through LETS; that would only give us a list of sixteen items. So what I am proposing is that we all offer six services each: that would give us a much larger choice of ninety-six items. That is a much better idea, do not you think?

["I guess so. When do you want me to send you my other five Offers?"]

I am actually working on the LETS directory now, so I would prefer to build your list up to six right away. I am sure it will not take long. Do you have anything in mind at the moment?

["Well, I like to get out on my bicycle as often as possible; I like the exercise. So you can put me down for ... say ... Bicycle courier ... and maybe I can teach members how to ride their bikes safely on the roads. ... I guess you would call that ... Road safety for cyclists.]

That is great, ... (Keith). Anything else you would like to add?

["Nothing else comes to mind."]

I have got a list of goods and services in front of me that I'd like to see in our LETS directory. Let us see if you can offer any of them. I will just read through the list and you can stop me when you hear one that appeals to you. Keep in mind that you do not have to be an expert with the things you are offering. I believe it is more important to be keen to help at whatever skill level you have, rather than being an expert at something you do not really want to do.

Then I read through the Jumbo Needs and Wants list *[copy follows after this phone script]* and added to his list of Offers until there were six in total.

Okay ... (Keith), now we have got six Offers that you will have listed in our LETS directory. If you would like to add more I can continue going through the list. Or do you want to leave it at six?

*["I think that'll do for now."]*

That is fine. Keep in mind you can always add or subtract items from your list at any time. In fact, if you ever feel you would prefer to stop offering something, please let me know straight away rather than refusing to help members who call you. Okay?

*["Okay."]*

Now, I want to get to the fun part. This is where I am going to try to find members to help you get more of the things you would like through LETS. And if our members cannot provide them, I plan to go out and see if I can recruit new members who can provide the goods and services that most of our members are looking for.

By the way, your choices aren't meant to represent your immediate Wants. I'd like you to choose items that you feel you may use now or at some time over the next year. So here we go ...

I had a photocopy of the Jumbo Needs and Wants list for every member, so I read through it again and placed a tick next to each item the member showed an interest in. There was no limit to the number of Wants they could choose, but I preferred not to accept any lists of less than six Wants ... I mean ... really!

Thanks a lot, ... (Keith). But just before you go, I want to know which of these Wants is the most URGENT. That is, which ones could you use right now.

["I do not have a lawn mower, so 'lawn mowing' would be a great help. And I would not mind getting 'piano lessons' for my daughter."]

Okay. I have still got another ... (fourteen) members to call. If any of them can provide those things, I will definitely get back to you and let you know.

Thanks for your time ... (Keith).

Bye

Whenever a member asked for 'lawn mowing' I gave them a guarantee that I would certainly find someone to do it for them. Why? Because lawn mowing was not such a difficult service to provide, and if I could not find someone to do it, then I would do it myself. Actually, it was probably the best decision I made.

Do you know how many lawns I mowed? I mowed so many lawns that my wife said, "How come you mow everyone else's lawn, but you do not mow ours?" And I said, "I am not mowing lawns: I am building a LETS group!"

That was exactly how I felt. I knew if I willingly helped members with that easy-for-me-to-provide service, they would reciprocate by willingly helping other members that asked them for help too, which was exactly what happened! After all, they were only offering services they were happy to provide, and now they had a sense of obligation because this nice man, James, had come and mowed their lawns. It was such a pleasure to see the transformation with the members' attitudes. It was the impetus we needed to attract more members into our group, and by the end of the year our membership had trebled to forty-five!

But, back to my lawn-mowing story …

It was true: my own lawn remained overgrown and a bit of an embarrassment. I could not motivate myself to mow it. The reality was that I hated mowing lawns … mine especially!

However, I really enjoyed the special treatment I got from the members whose lawns I mowed. I was always being offered tea and biscuits, and I also took the opportunity to share my vision of how fantastic our LETS group could be. I was truly on a mission to build C&D LETS into a strong and thriving group. My lawn, however, still had to be mown. So, I did what any other responsible husband would do in my position ... I got another LETS member to mow it for me!

So LETS not only improved my lifestyle by enabling me to get access to previously unobtainable services, such as massage, it also improved my lifestyle by allowing me to delegate, to LETS members, the chores I considered to be boring and mundane, knowing that those members actually enjoyed doing them: a win-win situation for all involved.

# JUMBO NEEDS AND WANTS LIST

This list of two hundred goods and services was compiled before I knew what LETS really was. Before my first trade with LETS, I thought LETS only catered for professionals and businesses. Nevertheless, by only mentioning some of the LETS-like services on my list, in the Arts and Crafts, Computer, Home Help, and Tuition categories, I was still able to help members add to their list of Offers. I almost chose not to include this list in my book, but I thought I would show you what could be achieved even by using such an inappropriate list.

## BUSINESS

**ADVERTISING:** Newspapers/Magazines, Radio/Television, Letterbox Drops, Billboards.

**PROMOTIONAL:** Graphic Designer, Photographer, Printer, Video Production, Signwriter/Neon Signs.

**COMPUTER:** Hardware/Software, Supplies/Accessories, Assembly/Repairs, Programmer, Operating Services.

**EQUIPMENT - Buy/Rent:** Mobile Phone/Fax, Photocopier, Other Office Machines, Office Furniture.

**BUSINESS SERVICES:** Secretarial Services, Business/Marketing Cons., Accountant/Tax/Finance, Solicitor/Debt Recovery, Serviced Offices, Window Cleaning, Carpet Cleaning, Removalist/Storage.

**OFFICE SUPPLIES:** Stationery, Rubber Stamps.

## BUILDING

**BUILDING TRADES:** Builder, Architect/Draftsman, Carpenter, Plumber, Electrician, Painter, Plasterer, Bricklayer, Tiler, Concreter/Paver, Fencing, Insulation, Heating/Air Condition, Carpet Layer, Cabinet Maker, Labourer/Cleaner, Handyman, Gardening/Landscaping, Rubbish Removals, Welding.

**BUILDING SUPPLIES:** Hardware/Tools/Timber, Plumbing/Electrical, Concrete/Plaster, Paint, Bricks/Pavers/Roof Tiles, Floor/Wall Tiles, Carpets/Lino., Windows/Doors/Locks, Plant Nursery, Swimming Pools, Kitchens/Bathrooms, Sheds/Rollerdoors.

## LIFESTYLE

**TRAVEL/ACCOM.:** Travel Agent, Air/Sea/Bus Travel, Car/Bus Hire, Hotels/Motels, etc.

**ENTERTAINMENT:** Restaurants/Fast Food, Cinemas/Theatres, Concerts/Sports Events

**HEALTH:** Gym/Swim Centre, Masseur, Naturopath, Chiropractor, Dentist.

**INSTRUCTIONAL:** Flying Lessons, Music Lessons, Computer Course, Business/SalesTraining, Personal Development.

**AUTOMOTIVE:** Cars (New & Used), Auto. Parts/Wreckers, Tyres/Wheels, Motor Mechanic, Auto Electrician, Panel Beater/Spray Painter, Car Detailing/Washing.

**PERSONAL:** Mens/Ladies/ChildrensWear, Shoes/Clothing Acc's., Jewellery, etc., Hair Stylist/Beautician.

## HOUSEHOLD

**FURNITURE, etc.:** Lounge Suite, Dining Suite/Tables/Chairs, Bedroom Suite, Wall Unit/Shelving, Wardrobes, Outdoor Furniture, Curtains/Blinds, Upholsterer.

**ELECT. APPLIANCES:** Refrigerator/Freezer, Clothes Washer/Dryer, Dish Washer, Stove/Oven/Microwave, Small Kitchen Appliances, Alarm Systems, TV / Video Recorder, Stereo/Speakers.

**OTHER:** Cameras/Video Cameras, Music Equipment, Sports Equipment, Records/Tapes/CDs, Books/Magazines, Gifts/Toys, Hobbies/Art Materials, Florist, Video Library, Picture Framer, Glass/Leadlight Repairs, Pest Control, Baby-sitter/Child Care, House Maid Service, Supermarket/Food Wholes.

# CHAPTER 8

## Recruiting

*"I refuse to join any club that would have me as a member. "*
*(Groucho Marx)*

## NORMAL ATTRITION

I knew that, due to various reasons, losing members was a normal occurrence experienced by any membership organisation. I found that, as it applied to LETS; some members simply moved out of the area making trading difficult, if not impossible; other members got new, or additional, jobs that robbed them of any free time they may have had for LETS trading; and the members who never traded at all – usually thirty percent of the members – did not renew their membership because they did not believe that LETS 'worked'. So, recruiting new members had to be an ongoing group activity to ensure the growth and survival of the group.

Various recruiting methods were used by LETS groups to attract members from their local community. Here are a few that worked well:

# LOCAL NEWSPAPERS

## WHAT'S ON SECTION

There was usually a Public Notices or What's On section in our local newspapers. As LETS was only of interest to local people, it was a waste of time and effort to promote our group nationally, statewide or even citywide.

We felt that people who read our local newspaper were excellent prospects for our LETS group; they were interested in their local community and would occasionally notice anything unusual – like a group of people in their area who traded with each other without the need for cash!

By promoting our LETS trading days regularly in the What's On section of the local newspaper, we attracted a small, but steady, stream of interested prospects to attend out trading days. They just about always became members before leaving the event. The temptation to join was too great when we told them, "Feel free to browse through the stalls. If you like something, you can become a member today and get it without paying any cash".

Apart from including all the relevant information in our What's On ads - day, date, time, address, contact name, phone number – including a 'hook', that is, something to tempt the reader to want to follow-up on our notice, helped increase the number of responses.

Helen Dew always promoted her trading days *[see 'LETS trading days' in chapter 5]* in her local newspaper. On Friday, April 4, 2003, she placed the following ad in the WHAT IS ON section of the Wairarapa Times-Age newspaper, promoting her Monster Garage Sale and my LETS presentation.

The hooks she used in both ads placed an emphasis on the international nature of both events:

*[Saturday, April 5]*
Green Dollar Exchange – Market/Garage Sale/Auction, St Mary's Hall, corner High and King Streets, Carteton, 9.30am-

noon, a fund-raiser for Helen Dew's conference in Germany. Contact Ruth 123-4567

***

Public presentation, at 1pm, hear James Taris tell how he has used green dollars touring eight countries and in Australia. Contact Helen Dew 123-7654

## FEATURE ARTICLE

Whenever I was shown a newspaper article featuring a LETS story, I wondered why more LETS groups did not take advantage of that option. It was only natural that the longer we were in LETS, the more likely it was for us to take LETS for granted. LETS, however, was still a very newsworthy topic – as I noticed on my travels around the world. In fact, I made it a standard practise to encourage LETS groups to approach their local newspapers to write a special feature article about LETS while I was in their area; this resulted in a published article most of the time.

The approach I preferred was to write a PR article and submit it to the local newspaper encouraging them to print it 'as is'.

Occasionally, my article was accepted. On other occasions it triggered an interest in the LETS group resulting in an interview being arranged with a journalist, and sometimes a photographer as well. The articles usually included reference to the group's most active LETS member, or a special LETS visitor, or an exceptional LETS trade.

Journalists were constantly looking for something … anything! … that would be of interest to their readers. Stories about LETS did that. My articles were about how LETS benefited its members, then I encouraged readers to find out more about the LETS group. A crucial part of the submission was to include a contact name and phone number at the end of the article. The story was then – almost always – published in the next issue of the newspaper.

## STREET FESTIVALS

Another excellent way to recruit new LETS members was through street festivals. Moreland LETS, in Melbourne, used this system quite successfully over the years. Each year, several street festivals took place in Brunswick and Coburg – our local community – and our group usually participated by setting up a Moreland LETS Information stall. The stall was manned by two members at a time … both occupying the stand for a two-hour shift. Their job was simply to hand out Moreland LETS Brochures to anyone who showed an interest. It was always low-key, relying on the eight-foot wide Moreland LETS banner to do most of the attracting.

## PUBLIC LETS SEMINAR

For my LETS Favours seminars, I always encouraged my hosting LETS group to invite the public as well.

I was particularly impressed with the way Timaru LETS, in New Zealand, organised the event for my presentation in April 2003. I felt they covered all the bases extremely well, making it a successful day. In fact, I offer it as a model for any other groups who would like to organise their own public event.

Here is the ad they placed in their local newspaper inviting the public to my presentation:

Timaru Alternative Trading invites the public to meet international traveller and speaker, James Taris, to a public meeting at the Caroline Bay Community Lounge, on Wednesday, April 9 at 2pm. James will speak on the subject of local currency and trading by individuals and how to enhance your life. Gold coin donation. Afternoon tea provided.

Most of the audience were LETS members, but we did get some guests through the newspaper ad – two thirds of which ended up joining; a very successful result.

My presentation was due to be given at two o'clock, so we went directly to the venue after lunch. Timaru Alternative Trading System (TATS) had forty members, yet we still got about twenty people to the meeting. The meeting was well promoted. Apart from the public notice in the local newspaper, a radio interview was given on the previous day as well.

A large A-board outside the main entrance directed the public inside, where 3 well-designed leaflets were handed to all non-members:

An A4 three-fold leaflet, **LETS Work Together – Trade with Timaru Green Dollars**, gave a very good explanation of how Green Dollars worked, and included a form that could be handed in, or posted, for further information.

An A4 two-fold leaflet, **Introducing Timaru Alternative Trading System Inc.**, gave answers to fifteen commonly asked questions about TATS.

A full-sized-A4 sheet, had the **Membership Application Form** on one side, and a 14-point list of **Terms and Conditions** on the other side.

On the table, alongside these leaflets, were a couple of good display signs:

**The Donation Notice:** "A Gold Coin Donation will enable us to continue our Green Dollar work in our community. Thank you." … was accompanied by a shallow bowl just inches away, eagerly waiting for those donations.

**The LETS Trading Day Notice:** "I am a local Green Dollar Member. Why pay cash when you could trade?" … also made its point very clear.

I did not know the newspaper had sent a journalist until I began my introduction and spotted her sitting in the front row, taking notes. A photographer came shortly afterwards. He took a number of photos and made me feel just a little self-conscious. After the presentation I learnt that they would be running the story in the newspaper's Lifestyle section.

## WHAT TO DO WITH NEW MEMBERS

Whenever our LETS group attracted a new member, I tried to get them trading as soon as possible. I did not want them waiting eleven months – like I did – before making their first trade. So, the new members got lots of time and attention on the day they joined LETS. After that they usually coped fairly well on their own.

The procedure I followed was somewhat like this:

### REGISTRATION FORM

Once they filled out the Registration Form, I asked for more details rather than just accept whatever they had written. It was easier to get the information from them at that moment instead of trying to track them down at some time in the future. Questions like ...

"What's your postcode?" ...

"Do you have an email address as well? Then we can email your LETS newsletter to you instead. That way we can save some trees and the cost of postage too." ...

"We like to have at least six Offers listed because we can never tell which ones you will be asked for. So, by having a longer list of Offers you are more likely to get trading much sooner."

I also took the time to get specific details for their trading terms. New members never had any idea of what they should ask in return for trading their goods and services. It was always a relief when they knew they had it all worked out before being contacted by a member asking for their help.

"How many LETS points per hour do you want? Usually our members ask for as little as ten points per hour for basic help, and then it goes up from there depending on their level of expertise. How much would you be happy to accept for your time?"

"Would you need any cash for cost of materials? It is best to let our members know if they need to pay for petrol, cooking ingredients, building materials, etc. before you commence the trade."

By getting their trading terms at the time of registration, I prevented new members from thinking they could ask to be paid partly in cash for trading their services. The ones that had that in mind then had to choose whether to trade only for LETS points or remove a particular Offer from their list.

## FIRST TRADE

My primary objective was to help new members make their first trade; preferably the minute they joined, or as soon as possible afterwards. I felt that as a new member they would find it hard to contact members for trades because, like myself, they may be afraid of being rejected. I wanted to help them overcome this hurdle by bringing them in contact with a member who would help them with their first trade. My hope was that after their first trade they would be hooked on LETS for life!

I started off by asking:

"What would you like to get through LETS?"

Then I followed-up with:

"Which one of these is the most URGENT?"

I always said, "most URGENT", not, "most IMPORTANT" because I wanted them to start trading NOW!

"You need your bicycle's brakes fixed and wheel realigned? Let me see, Keith should be able to help you with that. I will just give him a call and see if he can help you."

By making the first call for the new member, it took away the worry they may have felt about being rejected. It also made them realise it was quite okay for their account to go straight into debit rather than firstly into credit.

"Hi Keith. It is James Taris from the LETS office. We have just got a new member who makes leather goods: belts and bags, etc. His name is Steve and he needs some work done on his bicycle. It doesn't sound too complicated, just adjustments to his brakes and wheel. Do you think you would be able to help him?"

Once I tracked down a member who agreed to help – sometimes it took two or three calls – I handed the phone to the new member so he could make the appointment.

The new members were always impressed when they got such special attention, and if they had only listed a couple of Offers on their Registration Form, they were often motivated to go back to it and add a few more Offers to their list.

Finally, I encouraged them to meet as many members as possible ... as soon as possible:

"You will find our members are more comfortable trading with members they've already met. It is just human nature. The best way to meet our members is by attending our monthly LETS events. We have got a trading day on Sunday. It starts at one o'clock and finishes at four, but you do not have to be there for the whole time. I will be there, so I will be happy to introduce you to the other members. You will find more information about our last trading day in the current newsletter. My phone number's on the front page so give me a call if you need anything else."

Before leaving, the new member also received a membership card, LETS brochure, directory and newsletter. That was plenty of information for them to browse through in the interim ... between joining and making their first trade.

The next time I met them I asked:

"Have you made your first trade yet?"

If the answer was no, I said:

"I know it can be hard. Remember, it took me eleven months to make my first trade, but then, I did not know anyone who could help me. Anyway, I just want you to know I am still happy to help you make your first contact if you want."

They were pretty much on their own after that. They knew I cared about them and was available to help. The rest was up to them, and if they did not contact me again it was usually because they managed to handle it all on their own.

# CHAPTER 9

## Image

*"You cannot impress if you look a mess."*

*(James Taris)*

## LETS LITERATURE AND STATIONERY

When I had my photographic business, the studio literature and stationery I used, and circulated, was often the first representation of my business seen by potential customers. It was my studio's image on paper and gave my prospects an idea of what type of operation I ran. I wanted them to perceive my studio as being efficient, orderly and well organised. I did not want them to think it was inefficient, disorderly and poorly organised.

In the same way, the first thing I did with each LETS group I became involved with, was to look at the group's literature and stationery and see what impression it was giving prospective new LETS members. In almost every case, I was not happy with it – and the LETS committees were keen for me to redesign them.

The most common problems with the LETS material was that they were:

-inaccurate or out-of-date
-too complicated or too negative
-too hard to read because it was a copy, off a copy, off a copy.

I enjoyed redesigning the LETS literature and stationery because once they were completed, it sent a ripple of excitement through the group as each member saw an improved image of their LETS group. Of course, it made a positive impression on prospective new members too.

For a LETS group to function properly, I identified six essential pieces of LETS material. Here is the list:

LETS Registration Form
LETS Membership Card
LETS Transaction Book

LETS Brochure

LETS Newsletter

LETS Directory


In all the years I have been designing LETS material, I have always used Microsoft Publisher. Even though in later years I dabbled with more professional software programs such as Pagemaker and QuarkXpress, I found that Microsoft Publisher was much simpler to use and quite adequate for the purpose.

*Welcome to HamLETS, where we do not need cash because ...*
*we're bringing home the BACON!*


These designs are for a fictitious LETS group called HamLETS. As you can see, I have a bit of fun with it, both with the image and the group's motto. I recommend that LETS groups have some fun with their designs as well. I have found that new members are more attracted by the 'fun stuff' rather than the "formal (boring) or legalese stuff'.

## LETS REGISTRATION FORM

With my registration form designs, I included everything necessary to make trading simple for the new member and our existing members.

The account holder's agreement was also included on the registration form. I kept the clauses that attracted new members to join and removed the clauses that deterred new members. I had seen too many LETS agreements that were either too difficult to understand or too long and intimidating – like a legal contract. Our agreements were always succinct and inviting.

*[See Appendix for sample LETS Registration Form]*
Basically, the registration form gave us the new member's contact details and list of Offers.

**Contact details:** it was very important to get as many contact details as possible. Easy contact made for easy trading.

**List of Offers:** by having six numbered lines for the list of Offers section, it was easier for new members to accept that we really wanted them to list six.

I never included their list of Wants on the registration form. I felt it would compete for their attention with their list of Offers, which was of far more importance to us at the time of joining. The list of Wants only became important when I was trying to help the new member make their first trade, and if I was not present when the member joined, I could always follow-up with a phone call during the week.

Here is a sample Account Holder's Agreement (for HamLETS):

1. HamLETS is a non-profit organisation that provides an information exchange and recording service through which users can maintain a system of accounts for trading in local units called Bacons.

2. A Bacon shall be considered to be equal in value to a federal dollar. The Bacon exists only as an account entry. It never leaves the network and no bills or notes are issued. A Bacon is

created by a member in the act of obtaining goods and services from another member.

3. All accounts start at zero.

4. No interest is charged or paid on balances.

5. Account holders shall be willing to consider trading in Bacons. There is no obligation to trade. HamLETS does not set trading terms. All amounts (in Bacons) are set by members involved in trading.

6. Bacons will be transferred from one account to another only on the authority of the member providing the goods or service. Any transaction considered inappropriate or illegal will not be recorded.

7. An account holder may know the balance and trading activity of any other member.

8. Accountability for taxes incurred by account holders is the obligation of those involved in the exchange. HamLETS has no

obligation or liability to report to taxation authorities or to collect taxes on their behalf.

9. HamLETS make no warranty or undertaking as to the value, condition, or quality of the items exchanged.

10. While all efforts are made to maintain confidentiality, HamLETS cannot guarantee the confidentiality of information in members' accounts, nor necessarily be held liable for any breach of confidentiality.

11. HamLETS is authorised to levy account keeping fees on members' accounts. Currently this is 5 (five) Bacons per month.

12. Each member can trade down to a debit of 1,000 (one thousand) Bacons. When a member approaches this limit, their future trading activity will be reviewed.

13. HamLETS may act on behalf of the membership to seek explanation, account credit, or satisfaction from any member whose conduct is considered to be contrary to the interest of

other members. As a last resort, members may be removed from the network.

14. Any member whose account is in debit and intending to close an account agrees to inform HamLETS and make every effort possible to settle their account by bringing it to zero.

## LETS MEMBERSHIP CARD

*[See Appendix for sample LETS Membership Card]*

Membership cards were a great idea, although I cannot remember ever using mine. Maybe it was because I was such a high-profile trader. Nevertheless, they were still a good idea, even if it was just a confirmation that the person was a paid-up member of the group. The purpose of a membership card was to make sure that trades were only made between LETS members. However, I never heard of a case where someone tried to infiltrate a LETS system in order to obtain goods or services when they were not entitled to. But, come to think of it, it would definitely be essential in trading-day situations where the public browsed through the stalls along with LETS members, as was the case in New Zealand.

The membership card only needed to have the following information:

-LETS group name, address and phone number; -member's name, membership number and signature; expiry date of membership.

163

## LETS TRANSACTION BOOK

*[See Appendix for sample LETS Transaction Book]*

The best way of recording LETS transactions was by using three-section transaction slips. One section each for the Giver, the Receiver and the LETS Office. In that way everyone had a copy and there was no way for any mistakes or misunderstandings to occur.

As well as that, I found that including the instructions for using the LETS transaction book - on the inside cover - was appreciated by our LETS members, especially by new members.

The outside cover displayed the name, address and phone number of our LETS group, and the inside cover listed the Instructions For Use in four easy steps – as follows:

Instructions for using your Bacon Transaction Slips:

1 - Prior to the commencement of the transaction, agree to the amount in Bacons with the Giver (the person who is to provide you with the goods or service).

2 - When the time for transferring Bacons is required, fill in a Bacon Transaction Slip (all three sections) including, as indicated, the Giver's name and number, your own number as Receiver, the transaction date and the amount of Bacons to be transferred.

3 - Sign the Office's Transaction Advice, detach it from the book and give it to the Giver, together with the Giver's Transaction Record stub. The Receiver's Transaction Record stub, which remains in your Bacon Transaction Book, is your own record of the transaction and Bacon transfer.

4 - The Giver is responsible for delivering the Office's Transaction Advice to HamLETS Administration who will deduct the Bacons from your account, add them to the Giver's account and report this on your Statement of Accounts.

The transaction slips were in three parts:
[LEFT] Receiver's Transaction Record
[MIDDLE] Office's Transaction Advice
[RIGHT] Giver's Transaction Record

Each copy identified the date, Receiver and Giver (name and ID number), and amount of transaction. Description of goods or service traded, were also listed on the Receiver's and Giver's portions.

The LETS transaction books (which contained five, ten or twenty transaction slips) were usually collected from the LETS office. Some groups, however, offered them through their web site, which made it easy for members with Internet access to download and print them.

## LETS BROCHURE

*[See Appendix for sample LETS Brochure]*

The triple-fold LETS brochure was always an excellent tool for our LETS groups. It was a low-key promotional item that presented LETS to the general public. I saw some horrible brochures in circulation that I was sure did more damage than good. It was important to make them look neat ... with a good, positive message.

Designing my first three-fold brochure was quite a challenge. I had to keep in mind that Side One displayed panels five, six (back panel) and one (front panel); and Side Two displayed panels two, three and four (all inside panels).

Here is what I included on the panels of my HamLETS Brochure design:

Panel 1 – HamLETS, Grand Pork's Local Trading Network ... What is HamLETS? LETS stands for Local Exchange Trading System. HamLETS is a local trading network of businesses, individuals and community organisations. Members trade

167

goods and services through the exchange of LETS points called, 'Bacons'.

Panel 2 – How Does HamLETS Work? When you join HamLETS you pay a Membership Fee and open a Bacons account to track transactions. Members receive our LETS Directory (similar to Yellow Pages). New directories are sent to members as soon as they are updated. You can contact members directly and negotiate trades using Bacons. You can also supply your goods and services to other HamLETS members using Bacons. You will receive a statement at the end of each year with a list of your trading activities, although account balances can be obtained from HamLETS at any time.

Panel 3 – Benefits of Joining HamLETS ... Personal Benefits: Receive goods and services without cash. Update or learn new skills to offer to others. Community Benefits: Bacons stay in the community rather than travelling to a corporate office in another city or country. Trading supports local producers and improves the local economy. Trading creates its own community. Know your neighbours and like-minded people and trade with people you know and trust. HamLETS helps people to develop and use both personal and business skills.

Panel 4 – Business Benefits: Improve your cash flow or utilise underdeveloped resourses. Less wastage by trading your excess goods. Increase efficiency by trading services during off-peak periods. Receive an automatic interest-free credit line. Obtain business-related services and supplies without cash. Promote your business as supporting a local community group. Access new and unique markets. Create loyal customers. Generate referrals. Help extend the scope of your business.

Panel 5 – Who Can Join? Everyone has skills to offer. If you can provide a product or service to other people, you can earn Bacons to obtain other products and services! HamLETS provides you with an opportunity to help others with whatever skills you have. You could earn Bacons with: Skills you use professionally (e.g. You own a store, you are a book-keeper or a registered massage therapist) Skills you use as a hobby (e.g. You enjoy gardening, you make candles as a hobby, you like painting and re-decorating) Skills you used to use (e.g. You were an auto mechanic or a student painter in the past).

Panel 6 – Products & Services ...Here is a sample of some products and services offered by HamLETS members: Arts & Crafts, Accounting, Auto Service, Carpentry, Childcare, Computer, Clothing, Cleaning, Electrical, Florist, Food, Gardening, Graphic Design, Health, Home Repairs, Legal, Leisure Activities, Music Lessons, Pet Care, Transportation ...

HamLETS, 123 Spare Rib Dr

Grand Pork 4567

Ph: (098) 765 4321

## LETS NEWSLETTER

Because of their size and necessity for being updated monthly, LETS newsletters were my most challenging projects. However, they soon became my forte. Although they could be designed in quite a number of different and effective ways, I placed more importance on producing the most functional newsletter possible, where the emphasis was always on trading ... trading ... trading.

The newsletter format (for a small LETS group) was generally:

Page 1 – LETS group's name address and contact details; committee roles, co-ordinators' names and contact numbers; feature article

Page 2 – Events articles (report on last LETS event and promoting next event); office administration roster for following month

Page 3 – Member account balances *[we always circulated them so members knew the trading status of other members]*

Page 4 – New member block ads; Keen Trader block ads; amendments to existing member details

Page 5 – Offers section

Page 6 – Wants section

Page 7 – Helpful tips on trading

Page 8 – Other articles (including member submissions on Positive Trade Stories)

When the LETS directory was included as well, I added it as a four-page lift-out.

## LETS DIRECTORY

The most important item our LETS group provided to its members, however, was the LETS directory. Without it, our members were left in the dark, without any way of contacting other members to trade. If it was difficult to use, then our members would not use it. The following was the most effective type of LETS directory I ever designed. It was easy for members to use and encouraged them to contact other members to trade.

The directory was in two parts:

**Skills Directory** – alphabetical listing of all member Offers;
**Membership Directory** – numerical listing (by membership number) of all LETS members.

### THE SKILLS DIRECTORY

The skills directory was in category order, with sub-categories under each category. The objective was to help members find their Wants as quickly and easily as possible. If that process was difficult, or disorganised, it hampered the group's best means of recruiting new members and retaining existing members.

Initially, I tried to start with a standard set of directory categories. However, some of the categories I started with only had one or two Offers that I could place under them. In fact, a few categories had no Offers under them at all! So, when I prepared my first skills directory, I only had five or six categories in total. As our membership grew, and our listings increased, I kept the skills directory in order by introducing new categories to split overcrowded categories.

Here is an example of how I set out the categories and sub-categories alphabetically in my skills directory:

**ARTS & CRAFTS:**
Framing
Greeting cards and invitations
Photographer (weddings/portraits)

**BUILDING TRADES:**
Handyman

Labouring

Painting


**BUSINESS:**

Business consultant

Debt counselling

Delivery service

Office cleaning

Office work/administration

Time management

Typesetting


**COMPUTER:**

Computer assistance

Computer lessons

Computer operator

Desktop publishing


ETC.

All entries had:


-a detailed description of the Offer;

-and the member's number, name and suburb.

... And that was all! The rest of the information could be found in the LETS membership directory.

*[sample entries ... information placed in separate line entries under each category]*

---

(Under COMPUTER category)

**DTP Designing:** business cards, letterheads, with compliment slips, forms, brochures, flyers, etc. ... 077.Joe (Grand Pork)

---

(Under BUSINESS SERVICES category)

**Copywriting:** Advertising copy, sales letters, phone scripts, etc. ... 077.Joe (Grand Pork)

---

(Under MISCELLANEOUS category)

**Try me:** I am happy to consider anything else (for upto 4 hours) ... 077.Joe (Grand Pork)

---

## THE MEMBERSHIP DIRECTORY

The membership directory was in numerical order according to membership number. The objective was to give members the contact details and trading information they needed after identified them as possible trading partners in the skills directory. When that information was sparse, it discouraged members from taking the final step and phoning the member. But if it was very detailed, it encouraged members to make the contact with confidence.

All entries had:

-the member's membership number and name (first name or code name was OK)
-the suburb, phone number and email (if possible)
-list of goods and/or services offered
-their level of expertise
-trading terms

That made contacting very easy and trading more exciting.

077 - Joe (Grand Pork)
(123) 456 7890 joe@pig.sty
**DTP Designing:** business cards, letterheads, with compliments slips, forms, brochures, flyers, vouchers, etc. (No newsletters or directories. These take too long.)
- professional DTP service, only accepting work via email ...
*30 Bacons/ hour*
**Copywriting:** Advertising copy, sales letters, phone scripts, etc. - over 20 years exp. in business and sales, only accepting work via email ...
*25 Bacons/ hour*
*(min. 2 hours)*
**Try me:** I am happy to consider anything else, so send me an email and I will see if I can help ...
*10-30 Bacons/ hour*
*(max. 4 hours)*

# CHAPTER 10

## Committee Roles

*"Any committee is only as good as the most knowledgeable,*
*determined and vigorous person on it."*
*(Lady Bird Johnson)*

## THE 10 COMMITTEE ROLES

The most successful administration system we had, in the LETS groups I was involved with, was the 10-committee-roles system ... where ten members were voted into specific committee roles by the LETS membership. By giving the committee members specific roles and giving them the authority to perform their duties 'to the best of their abilities', the administration of the group got the freedom it needed to advance in leaps and bounds. Why? Because, rather than trying to run the group by bringing items for discussion to a once-a-month committee meeting, decisions could be made by individual committee members responsible for their specific roles at any time of the day, or day of the month. They carried out their activities with more enthusiasm, accepting praise for a job well-done and taking personal responsibility for jobs not-so-well-done.

Here are the committee roles that were allocated in the LETS groups I was associated with – along with their duties:

1 - Group Co-ordinator

2 - Meeting Secretary

3 - Cash Treasurer

4 - Promotions Co-ordinator

5 - Membership Co-ordinator

6 - Events Co-ordinator

7 - Newsletter Publisher

8 - Directory Publisher

9 - Website Webmaster

10 - Office Co-ordinator with Office Helpers

## GROUP CO-ORDINATOR

Over the years I noticed that the success of a LETS group, just like any other organisation, was usually the result of good leadership, that is, having a good Group Co-ordinator. What was our Group Co-ordinator supposed to do? ... NOTHING! Now that I have your attention, let me explain what I mean by 'nothing'.

The most common reason for a new LETS group 'dying' was the reluctance for members to replace a retiring Group Co-ordinator. And why would they want to?

The typical profile of a LETS Group Co-ordinator for a newly formed group was like this:

-had a passion for LETS;
-would seek help ... but would accept doing things themselves if they could not find anyone to help them, or their helpers were not doing their job well enough;
-thought about LETS twenty-four hours a day, seven days a week, fifty-two weeks a year.

So, one day they would get out of bed and say, "Gee, that was a stupid thing to do. I was so comfortable in bed. I do not really need this LETS headache anymore. Nobody helps me, nobody cares, and I do not get any thanks for it. And guess what … I do not care anymore either," and they would go straight back to bed again, getting the best sleep they had had since they started their LETS group … their LETS 'baby'.

Of course, when a replacement Group Co-ordinator was sought, the response was always the same.

"Are you kidding? Jill looked great before she started LETS. In the last twelve months she's aged ten years! Her hair was not always grey, you know."

"I could never do what Jill did. She produced the newsletter, and the directory; she arranged all the group's promotions; she handled all the membership enquiries and organised the LETS events; she kept all the member trading accounts, and goodness knows what else she did."

Yes, Jill had suffered from burnout, a very common problem affecting overworked, and overwhelmed, people in the workforce, businesses and organisations.

## HOW TO AVOID CO-ORDINATOR BURNOUT

To avoid this happening in our LETS groups, I made several recommendations:

First of all, the Group Co-ordinator should do NOTHING! That is, NOTHING ELSE but co-ordinate, or oversee, the activities of the other committee members. By sharing the workload with nine other committee members, nobody would ever get overwhelmed again, thus ensuring the survival and growth of the LETS group. In fact, because each committee role was reduced to only a smalltime commitment, whenever that role became vacant it was not hard to find another member to replace them. Actually, the best, and an often-overlooked source for new committee members, were the new LETS members. They were keen about LETS and could earn LETS points while performing their new role.

Our committee members were rewarded for their contribution, but not in cash, in LETS points. After all, LETS was perfectly placed to do that. Remember, LETS points were really just 'thank yous' for 'favours'. Why would not we show appreciation for the efforts of our committee members? Their efforts kept our LETS group running. If we chose not to reward them, then it was like using slave-labour, and no one wanted to be treated like that. In our LETS groups, the reward amounted to ten points per hour, which was the basic hourly rate asked by LETS members for their services. So, a committee member who accomplished his tasks in four hours was rewarded with forty points, while another committee member who required twenty hours per month received two hundred points.

All the roles automatically became vacant at the Annual General Meeting (AGM) – held each year. That allowed members to elect their preferred member for each role, though I cannot remember that ever being necessary. Most members were just happy to see a position filled. In fact, once a member had accepted a nomination they were virtually assured of getting the position. The reality was that several committee positions usually remained unfilled after the AGM. That was not seen as a problem, though. We just continued to advertise the vacant committee role in our monthly newsletter until it was finally filled. In the interim, the vacant roles were temporarily filled by the other committee members. Not jointly, but by several committee members taking on a second role.

So, back to the Group Co-ordinator's role ...

Apart from chairing a monthly committee meeting, the Group Co-ordinator was only required to keep in contact with each of the committee members to ensure they were able to fulfill their duties. That was it!

## HOW TO RUN LETS MEETINGS

Holding regular and productive LETS Committee Meetings is a crucial part of running any LETS group. Here are a couple of tips on how we ran our meetings:

1) Our meetings were open to all LETS members ... the more the merrier. In fact, members were even encouraged to participate in the meeting. Basically, each committee member gave a report on how their role was progressing. If they wanted any help, they asked for ideas, and any suggestions given during the meeting were just that ... suggestions.

As each committee member was totally responsible for their own role, they decided which suggestions to accept ... if any at all (although suggestions were usually greatly appreciated and accepted). Rather than being a recipe for chaos, it worked quite smoothly, avoiding many debates and clashes (typical meeting scenarios).

We did not worry about having a quorum in order to make committee decisions. As far as we were concerned, even if only two members turned up, all interested parties were present and would therefore make any group decisions that did not impose on any committee member's role. We felt that was a much better scenario than putting off decision-making for months on end if we could not get a quorum at our meetings.

2) We held our committee meetings at the same location as our LETS events, but they were held an hour earlier. There were several benefits from doing this. Firstly, it guaranteed we would have several more members at our events ... us! Secondly, it guaranteed that the venue for our LETS event would be open and members would not be kept waiting outside if 'the person with the key' was running late. Thirdly, it guaranteed that more new memberships would be obtained because guests would be greeted at the event by a committee member and encouraged to join.

## MEETING SECRETARY

The Meeting Secretary's role was limited to keeping minutes of the committee meetings.

Once the secretary typed up the minutes:

-one copy was filed away for future reference
-another copy was given to the Group Co-ordinator – so they could follow-up on all decisions made at the meeting
-and copies were also made for each of the committee members who received them at the next committee meeting.

## CASH TREASURER

The Cash Treasurer was responsible for all cash dealings. Usually, it was just a case of collecting the membership fees, banking them, and writing cheques for the purchase of postage stamps and office stationery. Fortunately, the LETS groups I was involved with were supported by Neighbourhood (Community) Houses and non-profit organisations, so we had no overheads. Our Cash Treasurer, therefore, only kept a very basic debit and credit journal. On my world travels, however, I attended several LETS AGMs where Cash Treasurers gave very detailed Profit and Loss Statements and Balance Sheets for the year's cash activities including: credits from grants, cash donations, and cash auctions; and debits from wages, rent, phone, electricity, printing and postage.

## PROMOTIONS CO-ORDINATOR

The Promotions Co-ordinator was our 'public face'. It was their task to increase the group's membership by promoting our LETS group to the local community.

Their role included all media contacts:

-placing ads that promoted our LETS trading days, or LETS get-togethers, in the What's On section of the local newspaper;
-organising interviews with the media;
-submitting editorial articles that promoted our LETS group;
-handling any outside enquiries regarding the group – other than membership enquiries;
-and ensuring we took part in the local street festivals by arranging for our LETS Information stall to be set-up, properly manned, and supplied with enough LETS brochures to hand out to the passers-by.

## MEMBERSHIP CO-ORDINATOR

The Membership Co-ordinator was the members' contact person. It was their responsibility to:

-help new members with their needs, especially with their first trade;
-help solve existing members' problems.
-act as Matchmaker for members who were having difficulty finding members to provide their Wants.
-contact members with large account balances either in debit or credit.

As trading was an essential part of keeping members happy and strengthening our group, we encouraged matchmaking.

If a member's account was over a thousand LETS points in credit, they were contacted by the Membership Co-ordinator and asked if they would like some help to find members to do anything for them. As they were often our most active Givers, we felt it was important to offer them help so they would not think we were taking them for granted. We saw no reason to restrict them from continuing to trade – as some groups did.

If the member's account was more than a one thousand LETS points in debit, the Membership Co-ordinator would look at their trading activity. If the member's account had been going in and out of credit regularly, they would be encouraged to continue trading. However, if a member's account had always been in debit, the Membership Co-ordinator's role was to contact them and help them take appropriate steps to reduce their debit level as soon as possible.

They could do that in several ways, by:

-increasing the number of goods and services they were offering;
-volunteering to supply goods and services promoted in the Wanted section of the LETS newsletter;
-promoting themselves as Keen Traders in the LETS newsletter;
-bringing goods to trade at the our trading day events;
-not refusing to trade with members contacting them for help.

When our groups were small, this role was handled quite easily. However, as the groups grew to hundreds of members, the role could have been shared between two, or even three, committee members:

-one for new members

-one for existing members

-one (maybe) for members with large debits.

## EVENTS CO-ORDINATOR

The Events Co-ordinator organised our LETS get-togethers and trading days. As we always held the events at our LETS office, the role focused purely on getting members to turn up!

Whereas LETS get-togethers only required the Events Co-ordinator to call the members and encourage them to attend, the trading days required more effort. Two types of members were required for a trading day to be successful: stallholders and browsers.

By getting members to agree to set-up stalls offering a diverse range of goods, and other members to provide hot drinks and food (biscuits, cakes, snacks), the Events Co-ordinator could promote the trading day more successfully to the rest of the members, thus attracting a good LETS crowd to come and browse.

If they also had someone at the door to welcome the members as they arrived at our event, it made the day even more welcoming and successful.

## NEWSLETTER PUBLISHER

I enjoyed the role of Newsletter Publisher more than any other committee role. I got to know the job extremely well. Monthly newsletters worked best because they coincided perfectly with our monthly LETS events. Our most common LETS events were trading days. They were held on the first Sunday of the month. So, the newsletter was sent out one week before the trading day. That resulted in a better attendance because it was a well-timed reminder of the event to our members. It took me about a week to prepare the newsletter, so the deadline for newsletter contributions was on the fifteenth of each month.

Even though I constantly advertised for newsletter contributions from members, I almost never got any. Nevertheless, I was prepared to write the entire newsletter myself if necessary, and whenever I needed any other specific information, I contacted the appropriate committee member to get those details.

The functions I wanted my newsletter to fulfill were to:

-encourage members to attend our next LETS event;

-encourage more trading between members;

-portray our LETS group in a positive way;

-build members' confidence in our LETS group.

# DIRECTORY PUBLISHER

The Directory Publisher's role was to promote the members' Offers to the whole membership. That involved contacting all members and:

-ensuring they were still willing to provide the goods and services on their list of Offers;
-encouraging the members to submit at least six Offers, and helping them choose additional Offers if necessary;
-including a detailed description of what was being offered and the cost in points (including any cash element for materials if required).

Then they prepared a two-part LETS directory:

-a Membership Directory displaying block ads for each member in numerical order;
-a Skills Directory displaying all the Offers in categories, listed in alphabetical order.

The LETS directory was the group's best recruiting tool. When a prospective member glanced through a well-produced and simple-to-use directory, they would immediately find items that appealed to them, making their decision to join also simple.

The LETS directory was also the group's best tool for increasing trading among existing members. When members knew the level of experience a member had and how much he wanted to provide the goods and services listed, it removed any concerns about contacting that member and virtually guaranteed their request would be accepted.

## WEBSITE WEBMASTER

Our Website Webmaster's role was to design and update the group's web site. That was done on a weekly basis. The directory was also on our web site, so it was the perfect way to keep our LETS directory always up-to-date. Our LETS directory was password protected, so access was restricted to members only.

Once the web site was created, maintaining it was not time consuming. I used to come into the LETS office every Thursday at two o'clock and make all the amendments in just one or two hours.

Having a web site was an excellent promotional tool for both prospective and existing members. It made our LETS group appear more established.

## OFFICE CO-ORDINATOR with OFFICE HELPERS

The Office Co-ordinator ran the LETS office with the help of a team of Office Helpers. The Office Co-ordinator prepared rosters for the Office Helpers (often new members) who made themselves available for shifts of four hours at a time.

The role of the LETS Office (Office Co-ordinator and Office Helpers) was to:

-handle all incoming phone calls, emails and snail mail;
-manage members' accounts by taking the Office Transaction Advices as they arrived and making debit and credit entries in the appropriate accounts;
-post newsletters and directories to members (photocopying, stapling, folding, licking and sticking postage stamps, posting out).

We always had two Office Helpers in the office, except when an Office Helper came for their first rostered shift ... then we had three.

***

I always concluded my LETS Favours presentation with the list of 10 Committee Roles and LETS members would come up to me afterwards and say, "That is what we have got to do. We have got to get more members to take on committee roles."

Every time that happened, I felt that I probably just saved someone from getting burnt out, or more importantly, probably saving another LETS group from dying.

LETS has been a wonderful discovery for me, and it has changed my life. This book has outlined how I improved my lifestyle and helped other members to improve their lifestyles as well through LETS. I sincerely hope you have gleaned some useful ideas from the previous chapters so LETS can do wonders for you too.

Happy trading,

James Taris

# APPENDIX I

## Starting Your Own LETS Group

*"If a man needs his appendix taken out, his gallbladder treated and some brain surgery as well, I do not think too many doctors would do the jobs simultaneously."*
(Bob Lavner)

## 6-STEPS TO STARTING A LETS GROUP

In my 10 years with LETS, I was involved in launching, or helping to launch, several LETS groups: Melbourne LETS, LETS Inter-trade and even LETS in South Africa. I was also involved with reviving a number of struggling LETS groups.

If I was going to start a LETS group today, I would use this 6-Steps to Starting a LETS Group strategy:

1. Find 6 core group (foundation) members
2. Create LETS group image
3. Promote LETS Information seminar
4. Hold LETS Information seminar

5. Recruit members

6. Start members connecting

## CORE GROUP

Form a core group of six foundation members for your LETS group. You must all be excited about LETS and totally committed to launching a LETS group in your area ASAP. Your core group members will most likely be headhunted by you from your list of RAFs (relatives, acquaintances and friends). You will need to talk about LETS to everyone, at every opportunity, and see if you can spark some interest and get some support from those nearest and dearest to you. Otherwise, you can advertise for a core group by placing a small ad in your local newspaper. That way, they will come to you.

LETS is not an easily grasped concept. So, in order to have your core group in the same frame of mind about LETS as yourself, make sure they have all read The LETSaholic Twist.

# FOUNDATION MEETING

As a core group you will hold a foundation meeting and give your LETS group an identity, an image and mode of operation.

You will:

-Vote for all committee roles, with some members taking on two or three roles temporarily.

-Choose a name for your LETS group.

-Decide on a business address for your LETS group. (This could be temporarily in a member's home.)

-Choose a name for your LETS points.
-Agree on the annual membership fees and monthly account-keeping fees.

-Agree to amount of LETS points awarded to committee members for performing their roles.

-Agree on days, dates, times and locations for ongoing LETS core group meetings.

-Announce that each member should begin performing their roles ASAP and 'to the best of their ability', with support and direction from the Group Co-ordinator.

-Choose a date for your LETS Information seminar.

-Ask the Promotions Co-ordinator to find a venue and (if possible) a high-profile LETS speaker for the LETS presentation.

-Nominate a member to design the LETS presentation material (posters and advertising flyers).

-Nominate a member to design the LETS literature and stationery. (ie logo, LETS registration form, LETS membership card, LETS brochure and LETS transaction book)

# PROMOTING LETS INFORMATION SEMINAR

Once a speaker, venue and date have been confirmed, begin a 30-day promotion campaign.

Your Promotions co-ordinator will:

-Photocopy and arrange for the distribution of at least 1000 LETS Information seminar flyers in local household letterboxes. (A 1% return is normal – for well-written and -designed flyers – so you can expect about 10 people to turn up from each 1000 distributed leaflets.)

-Put LETS Information seminar posters up in public places (library, community organisation offices, bookstores, etc)

-Send invitations to each core group member's list of RAFs (by email and snail mail)

-Send PR releases to your local newspaper, radio and TV. (Also make someone available for interviews.)

## LETS INFORMATION SEMINAR

Choose a weeknight (Monday to Thursday) for your LETS Information seminar so it does not clash with other functions.

On the night of the seminar:

-Get to the venue early for setting up.

-Only set up 20 chairs for your audience. It is psychological: if you set up 100 chairs and 25 people turn up, your event will look like a failure; but if you set up 20 chairs and 25 people turn up, then your event will appear like a great success.

-Have a member welcoming guests as they arrive and giving them stick-on name tags (first name only).

-Have another member at the registration table handing out LETS brochures and LETS registration forms.

-Get guests to enter their name, address and email in a guest book. These contact details can then be used to follow-up with other LETS news in the future.

-Start on time. If you want to start at 7.30pm, advertise the event as starting at 7.30pm ... free entry and coffee from 7pm.

-Keep presentation to 30-60 minutes.

-Continue with a Question and Answer period.

-Ask your guests to join tonight! (so you can begin compiling a LETS directory)

## RECRUITING

Recruit new members:

-Take payment for 12-month membership.

-Get list of 6 Offers (complete with trading terms).

-Supply them with a LETS Starter Kit.

-Ask if they would like to help in administration.

-Help match-make their first trades.

## CONNECTING

-Trading: encourage and support members daily.

-Produce your first LETS newsletter (including directory) – after 30 days ... repeat monthly.

# APPENDIX II

## LETS Starter Kit

Suggested contents of LETS Starter Kit:

-LETS membership card

-LETS transaction book

-LETS directory (as soon as it is available)

-LETS newsletter (as soon as it is available)

-LETS brochure

-The LETSaholic Twist

By including The LETSaholic Twist in your LETS Starter Kit, you can give your new members all the help they will need to start their LETS experience in a very positive way.

# APPENDIX III

## LETS Song

### LETS Song

James Taris © 1995

[Sung to the tune of YMCA, by The Village People.]

Hey there, there is no need to feel down.

I said, hey there, pick yourself off the ground.

I said, hey there, 'cause you feel down and out,

There is no need to be unhappy.

Hey there, there is a place you can go.

I said, hey there, when your short on your dough.

You can join them, and I am sure you will find

Many people who will help you unwind.

*Let us get together at the L-E-T-S.*

*Let us get together at the L-E-T-S.*

*They have everything*

*You can want in a flash.*

*And you can get them without any cash.*

*Let us get together at the L-E-T-S.*

*Let us get together at the L-E-T-S.*

*You can build a new home.*

*You can fix up your car.*

*You can live like a movie star.*


Hey there, are you listening to me?

I said, hey there, what do you want to be.

I said, hey there, you can make real your dreams.

But you've got to know this one thing.


No one, does it all by themself.

I said, hey there, put your pride on the shelf.

And just go there, to the L-E-T-S.

I am sure they can help you, God bless.


*CHORUS*


Hey there, I was once in your shoes.

I said, I was down and out with the blues.

I felt no one cared what happened to me.

I was broke, lost and so lonely.

That is when someone came up to me

And said, "Hey there, take a walk up the street.

There is a place there called the L-E-T-S.

They can help you back to success."

*CHORUS*

(Repeat CHORUS)

# APPENDIX IV

## Booking LETS Favours seminar

From 2002 to 2004 I travelled to nineteen countries, on five continents, speaking to LETS groups at every opportunity. With just a round-the-world ticket in my pocket, I travelled, basically, without money. This was possible because in every case I offered my speaking services for free to LETS groups that could host me for free. Depending on how long I stayed with each host, I did some of the following:

Gave my 90-120-minute LETS Favours presentation to their members, which usually had the following results:
-half the guests joined up on the day
-member trading increased by about 30%
-a couple of members volunteered to take on LETS Committee Roles

Promoted the LETS group through interviews with newspapers, radio and TV.

Promoted the LETS group by giving 15-60-minute LETS Introduction presentations to non-member organisations.

Redesigned their LETS literature and stationery (LETS registration form, brochure, transaction book, etc)

Reviewed their newsletter and advised of possible improvements.

Showed them how to make their LETS directory more functional so it could increase trade and new memberships.

Designed, or improved, their web site.

In return, the LETS group looked after my day-to-day needs, including:

Accommodation (usually staying with a LETS member – for about 7 days)

Meals (no restaurants necessary)

Pick-up from my last host and drop-off to my next host (or airport/train station/bus depot)

One day sightseeing tour of their town (by a LETS member)

Local transport (usually with a LETS member)

Internet access

Free time – to write my travel stories

Now I travel around the world quite regularly. If you would like to host me on my next world tour, please let me know of your interest by contacting me by email. *[contact details are on www.LETS-Linkup.com]*

# APPENDIX V

## Samples of LETS Literature

The following are samples of:

LETS Registration Form

LETS Membership Card

LETS Transaction Book

LETS Brochure

You can use these as a guide to design your own group's literature.

# LETS Registration Form

## HamLETS

123 Spare Rib Dr, Grand Pork 4567 ... **Ph: (098) 765 4321**

### REGISTRATION FORM

**APPLICANT**         (Tick one)   Individual _____   Family _____   Business _____

Name

Business Name (if applicable)

Address

Postal Address

| Province & Postcode | Date |
|---|---|

| **CONTACT DETAILS** | **LIST OF OFFERINGS** |
|---|---|
| Contact Name | 1 |
| Title | 2 |
| Phone (   ) | 3 |
| Cell (   ) | 4 |
| Fax (   ) | 5 |
| Email | 6 |

### HamLETS Account Holder's Agreement

1. HamLETS is a non-profit organization which provides an information exchange and recording service through which users can maintain a system of accounts for trading in local units called Bacons.
2. A Bacon shall be considered to be equal in value to a federal dollar. The Bacon exists only as an account entry. It never leaves the network and no bills or notes are issued. A Bacon is created by a member in the act of obtaining goods and services from another member.
3. All accounts start at zero.
4. No interest is charged or paid on balances.
5. Account holders shall be willing to consider trading in Bacons. There is no obligation to trade. HamLETS does not set trading terms. All amounts (in Bacons) are set by members involved in trading.
6. Bacons will be transferred from one account to another only on the authority of the member providing the goods or service. Any transaction considered inappropriate or illegal will not be recorded.
7. An account holder may know the balance and trading activity of any other member.
8. Accountability for taxes incurred by account holders is the obligation of those involved in the exchange. HamLETS has no obligation or liability to report to taxation authorities or to collect taxes on their behalf.

9. HamLETS makes no warranty or undertaking as to the value, condition, or quality of the items exchanged.
10. While all efforts are made to maintain confidentiality, HamLETS cannot guarantee the confidentiality of information in members' accounts, nor necessarily be held liable for any breach of confidentiality.
11. HamLETS is authorized to levy account keeping fees on members' accounts. Currently this is 5 (five) Bacons per month.
12. Each member can trade down to a debit of 1,000 (one thousand) Bacons. When a member approaches this limit, their future trading activity will be reviewed.
13. HamLETS may act on behalf of the membership to seek explanation, account credit, or satisfaction from any member whose conduct is considered to be contrary to the interest of other members. As a last resort, members may be removed from the network.
14. Any member whose account is in debit and intending to close an account agrees to inform HamLETS and make every effort possible to settle their account by bringing it to zero.

**I have read and undertake to abide by the terms of the HamLETS Account Holder's Agreement:**

| Signed: | Date: |
|---|---|

## LETS Membership Card

FRONT

**HamLETS**

123 Spare Rib Dr
Grand Pork, 4567
**Ph: (098) 765 4321**

BACK

MEMBER No. #          Expiry Date:

Name:

Authorised
Signature:

(Only this signature is acceptable on Transaction Slips)
**HamLETS**

Print 10 cards on an A4 (or 8-1/2" x 11") sheet of paper.

# LETS Transaction Book

## FRONT COVER

HamLETS

123 Spare Rib Dr. Grand Pork 4567
Ph: (098) 765 4321

MEMBER No. _____

BACON Transaction Book

## INSIDE COVER

Instructions for using your
**Bacon Transaction Slips**

1
Prior to the commencement of the transaction, agree to the amount in Bacons with the Giver (the person who is to provide you with the goods or service).

2
When the time for transferring Bacons is required, fill in a Bacon Transaction Slip (all three sections) including, as indicated, the Giver's name and number, your own number as Receiver, the transaction date and the amount of Bacons to be transferred.

3
Sign the Office's Transaction Advice, detach it from the book and give it to the Giver, together with the Giver's Transaction Record stub. The Receiver's Transaction Record stub, which remains in your Bacon Transaction Book, is your own record of the transaction and Bacon transfer.

4
The Giver is responsible for delivering the Office's Transaction Advice to HamLETS Administration who will deduct the Bacons from your account, add them to the Giver's account and report this on your Statement of Accounts.

## SLIPS

| Date | HamLETS | Date |
|------|---------|------|
| Gift received from (Giver) | LOCAL EXCHANGE TRADING SYSTEM | From my account no. # |
| Giver's Account No. | 123 Spare Rib Dr. Grand Pork 4567 | |
| Nature of transaction | Ph: (098) 765 4321 | |
| | Please deduct Bacon | Giver's account no. # |
| | And credit them to (Giver) | |
| Bacon given: | ( This voucher is for Administration use only | |
| | It has no value of its own and may not be used as a form of exchange ) | |
| | Receiver's Name | Receiver's Signature |

HamLETS
LOCAL EXCHANGE TRADING SYSTEM
123 Spare Rib Dr. Grand Pork 4567
Ph: (098) 765 4321
**Giver's Record of Transaction**

Date
Gift provided
To
Receiver's Account no.
Bacon received

Print horizontally – 3 each per A4 (or 8-1/2" x 11") sheet.

## LETS Brochure

Next page: 1) PANELS 5-6-1 ... 2) PANELS 2-3-4

## Who Can Join?

Everyone has skills to offer.

If you can provide a product or service to other people, you can earn Bacons to obtain other products and services!

HamLETS provides you with an opportunity to help others with whatever skills you have. You could earn Bacons with:

**Skills you use professionally**
(e.g. You own a store, you are a book-keeper or a registered massage therapist)

**Skills you use as a hobby**
(e.g. You enjoy gardening, you make candles as a hobby, you like painting and re-decorating)

**Skills you used to use**
(e.g. You were an auto mechanic or a student painter in the past).

## Products & Services

Here's a sample of some products and services offered by HamLETS members:

| | |
|---|---|
| Arts & Crafts | Food |
| Accounting | Gardening |
| Auto Service | Graphic Design |
| Carpentry | Health |
| Childcare | Home Repairs |
| Computer | Legal |
| Clothing | Leisure Activities |
| Cleaning | Music Lessons |
| Electrical | Pet Care |
| Florist | Transportation |

### HamLETS

123 Spare Rib Dr, Grand Pork 4567
**Ph: (098) 765 4321**

### HamLETS
Grand Pork's Local Trading Network

## What is HamLETS?

LETS stands for Local Exchange Trading System.

HamLETS is a local trading network of businesses, individuals and commercial organizations.

Members trade goods and services through the exchange of LETS points called "Bacons".

---

## How Does HamLETS Work?

When you join HamLETS you pay a Membership Fee and open a Bacons account to track transactions.

Members receive our LETS Directory (similar to Yellow Pages). New directories are sent to members as soon as they are updated.

You can contact members directly and negotiate trades using Bacons.

You can supply your goods and services to other HamLETS members using Bacons.

You will receive a statement at the end of each year with a list of your trading activities, although account balances can be obtained from HamLETS at any time.

## Benefits Of Joining HamLETS

### Personal Benefits

Receive goods and services without cash.

Update or learn new skills to market to others.

### Community Benefits

Bacons stay in the community rather than travelling to a corporate office in another city or country.

Trading supports local producers and improves the local economy.

Trading creates its own community. Know your neighbours and like-minded people and trade with people you know and trust.

HamLETS helps people to develop and use both personal and business skills.

### Business Benefits

Improve your cash flow or utilize under-developed resources.

Less wastage by trading your excess goods.

Increase efficiency by trading services during off-peak periods.

Receive an automatic interest-free credit line.

Obtain business-related services and supplies without cash.

Promote your business as supporting a local community group.

Access new and unique markets.

Create loyal customers.

Generate referrals.

Help extend the scope of your business.

## JAMES TARIS' LETS TOURS

This book is a comprehensive account of the information I shared in my LETS Favours Seminars with my LETS audiences on my LETS tours from 2002-2004.

2002 – Europe and South Africa LETS Tour

2002 – Japan LETS Tour

2003 – New Zealand LETS Tour

2003-2004 – World LETS Tour

You can read about my travel experiences on these tours in my books:

Global Quest for Local LETS

- My Europe, South Africa and Japan LETS Tours

Land of the LETS Green Dollar

- My New Zealand LETS Tour

400-Day LETS Odyssey

- My World LETS Tour

Email JamesTaris@gmail.com for further information.